Being a Man

By the same author

Angry White Pyjamas
Big Snake
The Extinction Club

Being a Man
in the lousy modern world

Robert Twigger

Weidenfeld & Nicolson
LONDON

Copyright © 2002 Robert Twigger

The right of Robert Twigger to be identified as the author of this work has been asserted by him in accordance with the Copyright, Designs and Patents Act 1988

All rights reserved. No part of this publication may be reproduced, stored in a retrieval system, or transmitted in any form or by any means, electronic, mechanical, photocopying, recording or otherwise without the prior permission of the copyright owner

First published in Great Britain in 2002
by Weidenfeld & Nicolson
an imprint of Orion Books Ltd
Orion House, 5 Upper St Martin's Lane,
London WC2H 9EA

A CIP catalogue record for this book
is available from the British Library

ISBN 0 575 07029 3

Typeset at the Spartan Press Ltd, Lymington, Hants

Printed and bound by Clays Ltd, St Ives plc

To Mark, Martyn, Peter and Nigel.

'Society everywhere is in conspiracy against the manhood of every one of its members'

Ralph Waldo Emerson

'The exact contrary of what is generally believed is often the truth.'

Jean de La Bruyère

9.02 a.m.

I'm driving past the immense white bulk of the hospital, which looms over the north of the town like shining marble cliffs – marble cliffs of impregnable arrogance and assurance – and I'm turning over in my mind an unnerving piece of information: from next Tuesday all patients will be barcoded. My wife pointed this out to me in the local free newspaper, which usually has two front covers, one paid for by a local car dealer and featuring the latest piece of polished metal aimed at men who think that more possessions will increase . . . well, something about their lives, perhaps happiness, perhaps a sense of security or well being. So not on the front cover, but tucked away inside, and in the subversive manner of such local papers it presents the news as a boon, as something we've all been waiting for, possibly even a tentative solution to the ever increasing length of waiting lists. My wife made a joke, imitating her arm being dragged repeatedly through a barcode reader, just like at the supermarket when your marked-down tomatoes fail to register properly. My wife was joking but it's she who will have to face the people behind the barcode innovation: in less than twenty-four hours she will be admitted to the hospital for a birth induction. As the time has got closer to this medical procedure its innocuous sounding title has ceased to calm and dissuade me that something bad is going to happen. I cling to the foetal picture of my child to be, squirming around in ultrasound scan land; he, and I'm convinced it will be a he, though we didn't ask, gave me the distinct and overwhelming impression that he would survive the pregnancy, he'd get that far at least. This intuition has helped curtail all my circling worries during these last nine months. Now the next stage looms and I'm a lot less confident. There is nothing left to think except, 'I hope it's over soon.' My wife is going at five p.m. to be 'induced'. They will introduce hormones into her body so that the baby she is carrying will be born.

My grandfather was away fighting in a war when his wife gave birth, and my dad was down the pub when I was born. Times have changed, things have moved on, and I will be there at the bedside holding my wife's hand in mine.

This is the Modern World

Let's face it, in the lousy modern world there is no such thing as manliness. There is no such thing as virtuous behaviour that only applies to men. It's better to get this one dealt with straightaway. I do not mean there aren't sub-cultures which are sexist, I'm talking about the formally accepted mainstream culture.

There are human virtues but there are no exclusively male virtues. Notions such as manliness are old hat now, best forgotten.

9.10 a.m.

I'm past the shining cliffs of the hospital, which far from being reassuring just remind me of all the sick people I've visited, and of all the reports of iatrogenic illnesses currently being treated. In this hospital 15 per cent of the patients are there because of ailments caused by being in the hospital – stubborn infections, mutant viruses, flesh-eating bacteria – they all lurk within the clean, shining exterior of the marble cliffs. But now I've passed it, and glad, like having passed a cemetery or a tract of new housing ruining farmland where you played as a kid, passed it and shooting down the offramp to Mothercare and all the other warehouse-size out-of-town megashops. I get in the wrong lane and someone toots aggressively. I look across and see a middle-aged woman in a brand new Volvo mouthing at me in a thoroughly unpleasant way. Jesus, I was only in the WRONG LANE FOR ONE SECOND, for Christ's sake. It isn't even ten on a Saturday morning and the rage is building. Other people's rage, I mean, not mine. I am determined to be very philosophical about driving, it's the least I can do in this age of madness. As she roars ahead I notice the yellow 'Child on Board' sticker in the back window.

This is my first visit to Mothercare and I'm not sure what to expect. I wasn't looking forward to it, but my wife suddenly remembered that we needed such things as nappies and one of those Baby Bjorn carriers that everyone says are so good. She reminds me that I was the one who suggested the baby carrier in the first place.

In the store there were very few people. Probably too early. I saw several blokes pushing pushchairs with their wives. A few kiddies running around. No one was shopping on their own. I went to the nappy section and was immediately confused. BUYING NAPPIES IS STRICTLY FOR FAGS, announces some weird and partially uncontrollable part of my brain. This part of my brain deliberately misunderstood the instructions on each brand of nappy so I ended up having to read and re-read each pack to make sure I wasn't buying something designed for an incontinent twelve-year-old. I then spent a long time deciding whether to go for a black 'Bjorn' or a tartan one. It was a really hard choice. Tartan was more cheerful, possibly more stain resistant, but would it ultimately prove to be deeply irritating? I didn't know. FUCK SHOPPING, says the dark side of my brain. I chose black. It all felt strange and false, as if I was undercover and, in fact, the nappies and the baby carrier were props to convince people I really was a fully grown man.

So, at the till, as they did their mechanical card swiping, I was thinking to myself, 'Everyone here must think I'm a dad with a kid at home just waiting to have his nappy changed. Everyone here must think I'm normal.'

Sex Please?

'Normal' now, confusingly, means two things. Either men with bulging biceps, less hair than the furze on a peach, and blotchy green and red tattoos, hypertrophically masculine, at least on the outside; or the majority of us, who feel no need to announce our maleness, beyond ticking the box marked M on application forms.

From time to time I think about getting a tattoo, but then the urge, thankfully, fades. And it isn't as if I've been in the Marines and have something genuinely macho to have needled in, like two mermaids cavorting with a machine gun under a royal insignia. I'd probably be reduced to having a dolphin or a Yin/Yang sign, something utterly unimpressive like that.

We live in a society that emphasises the similarity between the sexes, not the differences. This huge and remarkable change has occurred very recently, even though the causes of that change have been creeping up on us for centuries. Most places in the world outside the developed preserve of north-west Europe and the USA still prefer to emphasise the differences between the sexes, regarding one's gender as a major, rather than a negligible, fact of life. From such a perspective both types of 'normal' male, the tattooed tough guy and Mr Unisex, are distinctly abnormal.

Sexism becomes deliciously naughty in a unisex society. Hence the hypertrophism – the implants, the body building, the haircuts, the revealing clothes. The paradox of the unisex society is that, should you want to, you have to try that much harder just to appear 'male' or 'female'. In a sexist society even an effeminate man is closer to being a man than a woman. Even a butch woman is closer to being a woman than a man.

10.02 a.m.

At breakfast I re-read a section from *Aladdin's Problem* by Ernst Junger, a 102-year-old German writer who believed industrial capitalism was just a temporary phase. One phrase seems apposite: 'Everyone has a main problem. As soon as that is solved another problem is promoted to take its place, and that becomes the new main problem.'

I can easily see how worrying that you're 'not man enough' could become the main problem. It's not something that has its parallel in the female world. It doesn't make sense for women to worry that they are 'not woman enough'. Of course women worry about their appearance, how sexy they look, but not about how womanly, how essentially feminine they may be. Not women under fifty, not unless they're hiding it very well. The only time I came across such an open desire for femininity was in a young female guerrilla fighting in Burma who hid her broken nails and shyly asked me to send her tapes to learn French and copies of *Vogue* and other 'pretty' magazines.

I'm back home now, trying to understand how the Bjorn carrier works; no doubt when we actually have a baby it will be a lot more obvious how to string it together. I hate reading instructions but I sense child rearing will involve reading a lot of instructions on equipment and toys. I've given orders to my family that only wooden eco-friendly toys will be acceptable but already the garish yellow and blue plastic junk is piling up. People donate things to you that they found 'really useful'. Maybe kids really do need all this crap but I just don't know. I'm on a learning curve that's as steep and unforgiving as the north face of the Eiger.

Get a grip. I'm standing in the front room of our utterly conventional 1930s house, a house good for bringing up kids in, a house made interesting solely by the fact that it is in the last street before the wall that used to divide the middle-class private dwellings of the neighbourhood from the working-class council estate. The wall, which in photos looks like something from Eastern Europe or Northern Ireland was finally pulled down in the 1950s. The middle classes finally had to mingle with the people from the estate. Resentment is still supposed to linger, but the estate houses are now seen as good value by wealthy young professionals with shiny new cars, and slowly it is becoming more and more like our part of town.

The telephone rings and it's my friend Paul, calling to apologise for not coming to a party that some friends of mine organised a few days ago. He had wanted to come, but only if he could wear his normal clothes. The friends who were organising it had been quite harsh about this and had said no, he had to be in bona fide female attire. They knew that if they relaxed the cross-dressing theme then most people would weasel out. Paul hadn't turned up.

I should explain that attending a party in which I had to wear women's clothes had left me a little nervous and though I'm writing about it now I was rather sheepish when telling my father. Years before, I'd played a transvestite in a film and had no qualms whatsoever. Now I was older and less secure or getting more stuck in my ways.

It actually turned out to be a fantastic party and when thirty male and female transvestites turned up at the local village pub they stayed open until two-thirty in the morning just for our benefit.

Pretending to be a woman for an evening had given me a lot of new things to think about. I was surprised to learn that I actually almost preferred being a woman, within the circumscribed ambit of the party, because the main thing I felt, in my female persona, was that the pressure was off. I felt that the things I said could be witty without an edge. I could be verbal and clever and no one would mistake it for aggression or bumptiousness or pomposity or being boring. I felt freed up, light as the air in my little black dress, holding one of those triangular cocktail glasses with a tiny silver onion in it.

Paul is the most politically correct 'new man' that I know. When he told me he just wouldn't feel comfortable dressed as a woman it sounded strange, almost like a sexist comment. Oddly, it was my most un-PC friends that were most into the cross-dressing lark. Maybe Paul thought in some way we were taking the piss out of women.

Of course the men at the party were much more into being women than the women were into being men. There is something half-hearted and boyish about women dressed as men. It isn't nearly as funny as men dressed as women.

Paul tells me about his daughter, to whom he is devoted. He tells me that it felt weird leaving the hospital with a child only hours after his wife gave birth. 'I felt we weren't qualified to be parents,' he said. 'I felt we should have been on a special course and taken a test or something; it seemed kind of irresponsible of the hospital to just let us go with our child like that.'

10.05 a.m.

I asked Paul if he wanted to come to our barbecue lunch which we were are holding today, just a small thing, but both my wife and I have been gripped by a desire to live as normally as possible right until the . . . deadline. We will have the barbecue, wash up, twiddle our thumbs and early tomorrow morning go in stately pride to the gleaming cliffs of the hospital. I've already decided what I shall wear – white shirt, tie, nice trousers, jacket. I don't know why I should think that what I wear has any importance. Maybe I'm still gripped by samurai ideas I picked up when living in Japan, that a samurai has to dress up when he's about to do battle. Perhaps, with my paranoid suspicion of doctors and the whole medical establishment, that is how I perceive our upcoming appointment.

In the past an illness was just an illness, now I find myself subject to an increasing hypochondria – every illness being a potential gateway to death. And though I don't feel particularly old myself, I'm surrounded by men my age (thirty-five) or older who have started complaining of 'feeling old'. Those that don't complain of feeling their age say they don't feel 'hard enough'.

Others say that the modern world is 'too feminised', boring, safe, regulated and yet, what can you do?

The Things We Carried

I had my grandfather's old rifle manual from World War 1. I had a gas-mask case. I had a navy clasp knife with a marlin spike that was almost too stiff to unclasp. Losing that caused much anguish aged nine. Had a moth-holed battledress top. The bottom half of an incendiary bomb dropped on Nuneaton during the Blitz. A commando-style 'cap comforter'. A warrant officer's brass crown. Ex-RAF gaiters, always riding up over my skinny ankles. Aluminium mess tins – not army, but good enough. US army water bottle. A yellow Civil Defence armband from the 1950s. Nothing German if I could help it.

Things I was envious of: an air-raid warden's helmet belonging to a friend. An aluminium canoe with machine-gun rests and outriggers belonging to same friend's father. Anyone's father who had been in either World War 2 or the Korean war, or even National Service. My own dad had been exempted from National Service because he had a university scholarship.

Books: *The Wooden Horse, The Colditz Story, The Latter Days at Colditz, South By Java Head, The Guns of Navarone, HMS Ulysses* . . . and before that a solid diet of Famous Five and Arthur Ransome stories. Comics: *Hotspur, Victor, Commando Comics* with the dagger through the 'C'.

Poppy day, bomb craters, the stories of grandparents and parents, the disused Anderson shelter in my cousin's back garden, pill boxes, *Dad's Army*, how much butter a week you got during rationing, the first banana after the War and what my mum thought it tasted like, the weekly pilgrimage to the army surplus shop, making lookalike Sten guns out of wood with accurately drilled barrel holes, my friend's dad telling us you never hold the magazine when firing a Sten. Never mind the seventies, flower power, flared jeans and platform-soled shoes; for me and my friends it was all war, war, war.

We roamed the fields, built dams, made tree houses, dug holes fortified with barbed wire and linked them with slit trenches and tunnels.

Best of all was the digging of tunnels between the open-cast foxholes that covered my friend's back garden. Getting stuck in a tunnel could cause a panic – we'd read about that in *The Wooden Horse*. The secret was to lie still and relax – a stuck man takes up more space when tense.

There was nothing I liked better than digging big holes in the garden. In the end there were seven or eight abandoned workings in the garden; one, an evil smelling pit nearly twelve feet deep, with ever-present water in its clayey bottom. Despite my reading of the escape classics of World War 2 I never managed to solve the water problem.

Recently I had to dig out a large tree stump in the garden. It involved making a huge hole under the roots. I really enjoyed the work, sweating away in all that dirt. I was back with my friends, digging foxholes, tunnelling, preparing for war.

The Code

My nostalgia for things past included a fixation on codes of chivalry and courage; Scout's honour and being prepared to risk your life to save someone else. I never saw a river without imagining someone was drowning in it and waiting to be rescued, a railway track without working out how to save someone who had fallen in front of a moving train. For a while I was torn between a desire to be taller and pride at being four foot eight and half inches, since this was the width of the gap between the rails of a train line. Somehow I found this coincidence suggestive, perhaps it meant I would survive if I had to squeeze between the sleepers beneath a moving train.

I always knew the golden age had passed. I thought vaguely that it might have been some time in the 1930s – when boys still wore shorts and there were biplanes with floats and steam trains like *The Flying Scotsman*. I knew that the War ended this golden age. After the War there had simply been Teddy Boys, rising house prices, comprehensive schools and things getting worse all the time, not to mention my grandmother's favourite: the boys you thought were girls until they turned round and you could see they weren't, despite their long hair.

All the comics and old books emphasised courage and self-testing. I was frightened of heights, so it was up to me to cure it. If my parents took us to visit a church or castle I would often have to be taken down the perilous narrow stone staircases holding my mother's hand against the upcoming crowd. About two or three storeys above the ground was all I could manage. I kept clear of looking through the deep-set slit widows but, somehow, an internal altimeter buckled my legs after we'd ascended more than fifty feet or so.

When I was eight I found the highest tree in our garden, a willow with thick branches that sprouted thirty feet or so out of the crown of the pollarded trunk. I waited for a windy day, when these branches were bending large distances back and forth in the wind. I climbed the tree, slowly at first, three points of contact like the books said, to the top of the swaying branches and found that if I enmeshed my arms in the branches I felt increasingly safe. I even began to enjoy the sensation of being blown around. I was cured. The books were right: all you needed were courage, self-testing, honour, the old ways.

The Dive

I had less success learning to dive. One summer my friend's father tried teaching me. I had dived from lower down the diving tower but never from the high board – I always jumped. I was further instructed to open my eyes under water, which I never liked doing, even in fresh, unchlorinated water. My friend's father had dived off the bow of a destroyer during his National Service. A destroyer is very far from the water and diving off the bow, well, that's a pretty impressive dive. There was some complicated reason why jumping from a great height was more dangerous than diving, but I could never see it that way. My friend, encouraged by his father, dived off the top board. I knew that I could have dived if only I'd been forced, yet at the same time I was glad I wasn't being forced. Everyone said that it was all right, that even jumping was pretty impressive in its own way. When the talk came round to diving off destroyers all of us spoke as if such activity was for a previous age, that it would be foolish to expect such skill, or foolhardiness, in the present age. But I always wanted now to be as good as the past.

Sticks and Stones

I never liked going to the swimming pool either because a bunch of council-estate kids used to hang about the car park and throw stones at me as I locked up my bike. I never considered throwing stones back, instead I treated it as an exercise in weathering an attack, whilst locking my bike up in double quick time.

10.22 a.m.

The letterbox rattles imperiously – it's the estate kids calling to do the leaves, trim the bushes, wash the car or whatever other job I can think up. Today I'm too busy to supervise anything so I tell them to try again next week. One of the girls politely asks when the baby is due because her auntie is expecting a child too.

The main kid, whose name I don't know – I call him, to my wife, simply 'Fat Kid' – is a squat, doleful boy of twelve. Overweight, but not grossly so, he is the most persistent person

I have ever met, bar the odd Indian beggar. If I say I'm not using the car he suggests the weeds. If I say not the weeds he points to the hedges. Unless I'm very firm, as I was today, he'll spend all morning on the doorstep just thinking up new jobs.

One day Fat Kid turned up just as I was taking my usual walk around the block, the general-purpose walk I take to clear my head or persuade myself I've at least done some exercise. As I walked, he wobbled along keeping pace on his bicycle. He wouldn't be fobbed off. At first I told him bluntly: there are no jobs today. But he kept up with me, he kept walking with me chatting away, interspersing his general chit-chat with different job suggestions. This is when I discovered that he was bullied by hardnuts who lived in his part of the estate, which is why he didn't like the estate. They threw stones at him when he was on his own. Stone throwing hardnuts – somehow they could always throw stones far further and more accurately than us well behaved aspirational kids, even if we were better at throwing cricket balls than they were. The hard reality of a stone, they handled that better. And twenty years on, they're still throwing stones, at poor old Fat Kid.

10.35 a.m.

My friend Dave, whom I've known since we were at school, has agreed to drop his superior large barbecue off at the house. Right now I have to go into town to buy meat and charcoal. I can get there by a slight extension of my everyday walk.

The walk avoids the estate and takes me down a leafy avenue of large old houses, some still with the gnarled remains of fences made, I imagine, at the beginning of the century. The people who live in these houses like gardening and trees. Looking at the trees and the old fences I am calmed and reassured.

Today, as on most days, I see 'New Man' toiling up the opposite side of the tree-lined avenue. He is my height, has spectacles (oval instead of round, as mine are) and today is wearing a button down shirt, just as I am. There is one major difference and one minor difference: strapped to his front is a Baby Bjorn (tartan) and in it, just visible, is a tiny baby – girl or boy, I haven't really considered. The minor difference is that on cold days he wears a Peruvian knitted cap with dangly bits over the ears, as worn by peasants in the High Andes.

Some days I walk on the same side of the road as New Man and this entails moving slightly out of the way. He gives me an apologetic smile and I grin back. Not for us the hostile stare of the hormonally challenged.

I have felt rather superior to New Man, until recently. I used to say to myself – why can't his wife carry the nipper? But now, as zero hour approaches, I know that I, too, will soon be 'Bjorned' up. Thanks to my extensive reading on childcare in the upper Amazon I have become convinced about the therapeutic effect of carrying children. Except I don't really want to be the one doing it. Neither does my wife. She isn't so keen on lugging the baby everywhere on her hip like a naked member of the Jivaro tribe. Reality is now dawning brightly around the curtains I have chosen to draw – I now glimpse myself in New Man, how he may even resent carrying the kid, think that it is his wife's job, but does it out of a conviction that his feelings are secondary to the child's wellbeing.

Sometimes, on colder days, as well as the hat, New Man wears a big overcoat which partially obscures the little figure clinging to his chest, and passersby do not notice he is 'with child' until he's past and the baby is gurgling and sticking his fat little hand out from behind the curtains of his coat.

Just as I'm level with New Man, sneaking a glance across at him as he strolls along talking to his baby, a group of teenage girls come spilling out of one of the houses. He waits patiently for them to get out of the way and the girls take this as their due, hardly noticing him and his baby. This is unusual. In most cases people are very keen to give New Man right of way. Teenage girls in a giggling hurry are an exception. Everyone else is respectful, everyone else wants to show how much they care.

The child has become the final benchmark, the ultimate testing ground, the ethical teaser, the moral marker – we can agree on nothing in this world, nothing is universal except we MUST NOT HARM KIDS. Kids have replaced heaven as the ultimate destination of our quintessence. Kids carry our genes, which are us, if you choose to believe popular science. Kids are the future.

People want to show they care, people in the street get out of your way if you have a kid. Cars stop, virtually screech to a halt to let you cross, do them the honour of crossing in front of them.

People also want to make contact. They yearn to make contact with other people, but they fear rejection. Kids circumvent this, especially babies in carriers. Men and women, but especially women who have or have had babies, reach out and hold New Man's kid's hand; they happily gurn back at him, even imitate his abrupt yelp of approval. Old people at the bus stop see the papoose and say to him, 'That's the way to travel!' And all the time the kid is rewarding people with his smile, his non-judging smile that means contact at last.

Only the very old, if alone, still ignore both the baby and New Man. Old women, the tidy kind in thick uncomprehending glasses, make their way past him, as if someone does not belong.

Tiny kids are a passport to a friendlier, more open, more trusting world. This is nice if you have kids, less nice if you don't. Some pubs still don't want screaming kids interrupting drinking time, and who can blame them, but in general kids are most welcome most places now.

Where are the men's places where kids are not welcome? The warzone, the workshop, the sea during a storm. More obviously, too, the lap-dancing bar, the porn shop, the brothel.

When I watch the way New Man chats with people in the street it seems like a return to the 1950s. Everyone wants to talk, and I like that. But despite all this, I still think there is something odd going on, that he is going against nature in some way. It is true, one cannot run or fight with a child on one's back. One must rely on the goodwill of others. Maybe men should not have to rely overmuch on the goodwill of others. Maybe that undermines some deep sense of self-reliance. In martial arts, in order to build the right ready-for-anything attitude, people speak of being prepared to die at any minute. You might die carrying a kid, but you won't die fighting, you'll die pleading.

Whichever way I twist something in me disapproves of the child carrier.

Youth is the New Masculinity

We live in a society that actively promotes safety over danger, pleasure over pain, dependence over self-reliance, living for the future rather than for the moment. Old age, too, is equated with safety, avoiding pain, avoiding risk and danger, taking it easy in a safe haven. The young react against this and create their own culture of excess, thrill seeking, irresponsibility, lack of planning. It makes sense to say that the new division of society is between the young and the old. This has replaced the old division between male and female.

More 'backward' cultures, those in Latin countries, Japan, or my wife's birthplace, Egypt, still conform far more to the old m/f dichotomy. This seems to benefit men more than women, but that isn't my point. In these old style homocracies (dangerous word that) it is possible to see men aged 80 with a dignity and bearing that is increasingly rare in the Anglo-Saxon world. 'I'm a man' their dignity and bearing pronounces, rather than 'I'm old'.

It's an idea I want to return to, but I think there are many consequences to living in a unisex society. For one thing, we become like grouperfish, starting life as male and then undergoing a sex change half way through. In this instance I'm equating male with young and female with old, using traditional ideas about what constitutes typically male and typically female characteristics. Men, traditionally, were thought to be the more outgoing, in need of testing and danger, the protector, the cool head in a crisis. Women were thought to be the nest builder, the provider of a home environment, the watcher over children, keeping them out of danger, the planner for the future. These now deeply unfashionable ideas are attached without comment to the elderly. It is considered natural and right that the elderly should concern themselves with safety, homebuilding, planning for the future, avoiding all risk.

That youth is the new masculinity can be tested by comparing the way men are regarded in a sexist country such as Egypt and the way young people are regarded here. In Egypt men are always referred to for their opinion, even if it's banal, simply because they are men and culturally thought to have their fingers on the pulse of what is important. Their opinion is sought and then carefully ignored by women who have their own agenda. Likewise 'youth' is always being consulted in the West. Finding out what young people want is considered a necessary part of any campaign, sales drive, brainstorming session. Yet even a moment's reflection would reveal that young people, as a group, are no more privileged than men, as a group, with valuable insights. In many ways the young are more conservative, less creative and less flexible than their elders – but like men in the Middle East they're not embarrassed to tell others what should be done.

10.45 a.m.

I shop at a particular butcher's because they stock organic meat. It may not taste any better but it certainly makes me feel better when I eat the stuff. Despite complaining about the lack of risk in everyday life, the risk of BSE, CJD, MCF (Malignant catarrhal fever) or F&M (foot and mouth) is one risk I'm happy to do without.

In the butcher's there is a nervy middle aged man ordering meat for a complicated recipe.

Nervy Man: Have you got any shoulder of pork?
Butcher: You mean spare rib. Of course.
Nervy Man: Have you any bedpiece of beef?
Butcher: You mean thick flank. How much?
Nervy Man: And have you any single loin chops?
Butcher: You mean lamb cutlets. Yes.
(big pause)
Nervy Man: That's not what my recipe book calls them.

Is the butcher lying or is the Nervy Man an incompetent fool? We just don't know. In fact all of us waiting to get served are on tenterhooks to find out. Nervy Man seems unaware that he is implying that he trusts his recipe book more than the butcher, and everyone in the shop knows this, and knows it is foolish since the butcher is obviously a professional and yet can we trust professionals these days?

Almost every time I go into the butcher's it seems to be full of middle-class men inexpertly buying meat. I fantasise that buying meat has replaced hunting for it, or maybe meat buying has become the least effeminate form of food shopping, now that men have to share everything.

I put the meat in my small rucksack and head to the garden shop to buy charcoal. I deliberately choose the stuff which hasn't been doused in napalm-derived chemicals. Carrying the charcoal in both arms out of the shop I catch a glimpse of 'Low Serotonin Man'. He is riding a knackered looking bike along the pavement smoking a cigarette. He sees me and our eyes meet for just a second before he is past. LSM is about twenty or so, with a face that looks as though someone has squashed his jaw upwards and his brow downwards. He is liberally pock-marked and his expression has the classic deprived look of the young(ish) offender. His hands are covered with botched blue ink tattoos, self-administered. I once shouted at LSM when he had been climbing over the fence of next door's back garden, looking for something to steal, but he just turned tail and legged it. Since then I see him quite often, but I say nothing and he just gives me a dirty look. A neighbour told me that the police know he's responsible for half the trouble caused in the area but they can't prove anything.

Back at the house Dave has left a message saying that he can't drop the barbecue off until later that morning. I listen to the answerphone message, annoyed at myself for still feeling unsettled by the sight of that ugly face.

The Knowledge

It wasn't that I was bullied at school, that didn't happen, it's just that I developed a way of acting and talking so as not to attract adverse attention. If I'd wanted more fights I could have been more 'myself'. One area in which originality wasn't penalised was doing crazy things, dangerous things, stuff that even the hardnuts didn't do. One night I broke into the school and climbed on to the roof of the highest block and fixed a white flag to the teetering lightning-conductor pole that stood up from the ridge. The next day the hardnuts speculated, knowingly, how it had been done and I hugged to myself gleefully the knowledge that they hadn't a clue.

The Rock

It was a sunny day and the beach was steep sloped, covered in layers of smooth, massive pebbles. I was fourteen years old and a strong swimmer. I'd get to that rock easily, far out in the bay with a few gulls, tiny white smudges rising and then abruptly falling down to the sea around it.

I set off swimming breast stroke, the best stroke for long

distance, less tiring. Captain Webb, the first man to swim the Channel, swam breast stroke. The sea was not warm, but neither was it so cold as to make swimming impossible. After a few minutes' hard swimming I ceased to notice the sea's temperature.

We were on holiday in Brittany and every day we came to this almost deserted rocky beach, and every day I looked at the rock, the rock island, I called it. If I could swim all the way to the rock island I would have succeeded in some obscure but very necessary way. Getting there would be like the Famous Five visiting Treasure Island. Or like John swimming around Wildcat Island in *Swallows and Amazons*.

When I could no longer feel the bottom I looked over my shoulder to check my parents up at the beach encampment of towels and wind screens tethered to rocks. No one was looking. I swam on.

For a long while it seemed as if I was just going through the motions, bobbing up and down, hit in the face by the odd windblown breaking wave, remaining stationary in the big sea. But when I looked back at the beach I could see I was a long way out.

Sometimes I swam with my fingers splayed, just for a change. Other times I made them into an efficient paddle shape – it didn't seem to make much difference to my slow bobbing progress

It now seemed as if the rock island was getting larger more quickly and the beach was receding less quickly. The sea was colder and greener and I was out beyond the two rocky headlands.

The rock loomed as I approached, quite high and black and splashed with wet. When I was under its shadow I could feel the sea taking hold of me with a new vigour. I touched the sharp side of the rock like a swimmer touching the end of the pool before a turn. It hadn't been so difficult, after all. I hung on to the dark slimy strands of seaweed, anxious to keep my toes clear of the underhanging rock. It was a salty, dark, rank dampness and my chest was all scratched when a heavy movement of water lifted me up against the rock's face.

I made my way around the rock looking for a toe hold, the half-dry, half-foetid seaweed getting in my face. At the far side I found a way up to the sharp pitted top and waved at the land, too far out by now to be seen except through binoculars, or by someone with excellent vision, like my father. I thought then that my parents would probably be 'worried'; they often were.

My father had grown up in India during and after World War 2. His tales of childhood were fantastic expansive tales worthy of any children's adventure book. Mine were paltry by comparison, hopelessly cramped, low budget grainy rip offs of the real thing. He had been taken on a day's hike into the jungle by Naga headhunters when he was eight, walked twenty miles along trails and drunk wild tea brewed in the end of a piece of bamboo. He'd slid down the side of a bomb crater at the site of the battle of Kohima and cut his hand open on barbed wire entangling a Japanese corpse. Getting serious cuts, he led me to believe, was the sign of a real childhood. I didn't like cuts, hated them, in fact, and saw this as further proof that my childhhood wasn't up to the mark. When my father came to England to boarding school, when he was thirteen, he and his brother had had thirteen fights in the first week. I'd had less than that in my whole time at school, plus I didn't even go to a boarding school which I knew would be much more exciting than a boring day school. My mother strongly disapproved of fighting and said so. My father would agree and then tell me these stories.

I was on the rock and I waved, trying to put the probable ire of my parents out of mind. Then I jumped in and started back.

This time I entered that zone where you seem to be making very slow progress much sooner. I lined myself up with the two headlands and, looking no further ahead than a few metres, I bobbed up and down, pawing at the water in a trancelike state.

I looked up after a while – it can't have been more than ten or fifteen minutes – and without thinking about it checked my position with regard to the two headlands jutting out. But instead of slow progress this time I really had got nowhere at all. With a horrible gut surge of fear I saw that for ten hard minutes I had simply kept level with the current taking me out to sea. And when I got so tired I couldn't swim I knew I would be drawn out to sea like those kids who get lost on inflatable mattresses, except I wouldn't even have an inflatable mattress.

I made my arms surge, my legs kick hard against resistance, instead of their previous finlike slip-slipping through the water. All exertion was directed forward, checking the headland every few seconds, my senses boosted to a whole new level with panic energy.

I was still too far out to be seen as in trouble, unless someone was checking my no progress. If my great boiling fish impersonation should fail, then I would be washed away, or drowned, at least in DEEP TROUBLE and without anyone knowing about it.

The new energy came from knowing that I had transgressed some special boundary. I was now on serious turf. It was no longer a game. Serious turf, I knew, had been the proper arena for adults until my parents' generation. Serious turf meant wars, danger, extremes of weather, illness, death, the sort of thing that happened quite often in the 1930s. Intuitively I knew that this place was elsewhere than here; Europe in the last quarter of the twentieth century.

I still seemed to be getting no closer to the beach, despite all this new effort. How long could I keep it up? I did not think about dying because I knew such thoughts would be no use to me. Instinctively I knew I had only energy for useful thoughts.

But just when I was beginning to flag I administered a shock of fear to myself by imagining myself drowning, the physical feel of my mouth filling with water. This worked like a hypodermic full of adrenaline, and when I flagged again I injected myself with fear again.

Now I began, I thought, imperceptibly almost, perhaps, to move against the current.

But I was tiring. My arms protested thinly against the water, hands open or splayed, cutting not much grip against the waves. And cold. I had the odd sensation of cooling as I worked harder, instead of getting warmer.

But definitely, now, my 'realistic' pessimism could not disguise the fact, I was moving again towards the beach. I was beating the current. Important not to get overconfident, though, so I told myself I wasn't safe until I was standing on dry land again. I thought for a brief moment about the underwater stepping stones that had saved one character swimming in open sea in *Island of Adventure* by Enid Blyton. He had been out of his depth and tiring, just as I was. There would be no stepping stones today, I knew that.

Half way there now, well inside the bay. The current pulling against me was slacker here. I still used fear to spur me forward. Less than two hundred metres from the stony beach I saw my father perform the shallow dive he did so well and power towards me using the crawl. He was egregiously angry. I might have drowned, he said, several times. Everyone had been worried. They had only noticed me on the way back. They had only noticed me when I was safe again. My father escorted me like a destroyer bringing in a wounded fishing boat. Him sharking and circling around, me lumbering forward with my breast stroke.

At the beach my father still red faced and annoyed stalked up the steep slope of cobbles. I hid the fact that I could not stand and, as the water grew shallower, I swam until I grounded out on knees and elbows. Getting clear of the back suck of the sea was a last huge effort. I lay in the weak sun just clear of the outfurthest wave runs, my heart sounding quickly and quietly inside my body. After ten minutes I moved; still not able to stand

I crawled instead on hands and knees, lying down sometimes to rest on the plate-sized warm pebbles.

More admonition awaited me at the beach encampment of tartan rugs, edges pushed down into the sand and the wind shield, a canvas contraption secured by guylines on to large rocks. I dressed silently. Pulling jeans over cold flesh that retained the dent after a thumb was pushed into the thigh. It was a sunny day but I even pulled my waterproof cagoule over my jersey and shirt. On my feet were socks and shoes. And still I was cold, bone cold. It wasn't till late that evening after both lunch and dinner and sitting by the open fire in our holiday house that, at last, I was warm again. Of course, I never told anyone why I had done it.

Schooldays

The school I went to, owned and run by the state, wasn't a bad school, by any standards, but there was nothing about it that could make you proud of having been there. Even the rugby team, which I captained briefly, sometimes went for years without a single victory. I was envious of people who went to well-known private schools, but when I met them at university I discovered that they, too, had their own grudges. This left me unwilling to attack one system in favour of another. We had our slags and hardnuts, they had their snobs and psychological bullies.

Adidas bags were the thing at school – the bigger the better, one boy had a monster-sized cricket bag. He never used to carry more than his sandwiches in it since he was too cool to remember his books. I had a satchel – old satchel foot, that was me – and I yearned for the anonymity promised by an overpriced plastic carryall carrying the Adidas logo. Trousers were judged by the number of buttons at the waistline. Again, the boy with the enormous bag also had four-button trousers. Mine had only one button, with only a slight flare and no patch pockets; accessories I acknowledged as necessary but also privately disliked. The bike was also important – ten-speed if you were middle class; with cowhorns and a chopper saddle if you weren't. At sixteen the hardnuts who had ruled the school by violence and threats of violence suddenly were overtaken by boys who could afford mopeds and, a year later, motorcycles. The first moped had to be either an R reg Fantic or Yamaha FSIE, the last year they made sixty mile an hour unrestricted 50cc bikes. At seventeen the correct choice was a Yamaha LC250 and at eighteen you got a car, or a van. The rite of passage had very clearly been transmuted from an experience one underwent to a thing one possessed. This wasn't questioned, indeed, in the manner of young people the world over, it seemed entirely logical that most boys (always boys) should want a motorbike identical to that owned by everyone else. I found myself eagerly taking part in energetic discussions concerning the virtues of one motorbike manufacturer over another even though I had no money nor even much interest in owning one for myself.

But owning things was what counted. One boy, whose parents had died, owned his own house – what more genuine sign of adulthood could there be? Only off the record, in the margins, as a laugh or a good crack, did the challenge and the test assume any importance.

Driving Test As Rite Of Passage

I'd passed my driving test but I really needed glasses to drive, especially at night, and I'd left them at my best friend Pete's house. So when I was allowed to drive Pete's Escort to the pub I was nervous and careful. Not so after eight pints of warm bitter beer and many visits to the loo. Peanut, who had done most of the talking, was on his tenth of lager, but showed no sign of it. Peanut was a thick-armed farm labourer with blond hair somehow reminiscent of Woodstock in the *Peanuts* cartoon. Maybe that was why he was called Peanut. He had a hard, flat chest and in a fight preferred to bear-hug his opponent. The previous week he had bear-hugged a man and broken three of his ribs. Not that Peanut was a hardnut, I could see that; it was just that drinking in rural towns sometimes involved bear-hugging people who were rude. I sensed that in this agricultural backwater (I had travelled to see Pete, who lived deep in the Gloucestershire countryside) my city-learned rules did not quite apply. I was only eighteen, and careful to observe the etiquette, watching my friend Pete, who had dropped out from doing A levels and taken up doing contract ploughing and helping during the harvest in order to earn enough to keep his elderly Ford Escort on the road.

Peanut's car was a fiddled-with Ford Anglia with a Confederate flag on the bonnet and 'Colonel Bogie' playing on the horn, which was delivered through a copper cable a quarter-inch thick to get the ampage and the volume.

After his ten pints Peanut suggested, in a light-hearted tone, that we attempt a ton down the back lane a mile or two from the pub. That this was foolhardy was never even discussed; that it might be difficult and dangerous never referred to. The talk instead focused on the particular tweaks the engine had received, the state of the tyres, how the brakes were still a little sticky. In careful and measured tones Peanut and Pete outlined the necessity of the test and I thought for a few horrible minutes that I would be forced by the sheer momentum of the discussion to actually take the wheel of Peanut's car. This was not required, each man having to drive his own car unless he was a very close friend, as Pete and I were. The car I could see was part of the test. One had to have one capable of doing the magic 100 m.p.h., and Pete's wasn't up to it though he was keen of course to upgrade to something faster, perhaps a Capri or souped up Dolomite. I knew Pete very well, I had known him since we were seven, and I could tell he was not very keen on this driving stunt. But both of us knew we were locked into something that involved not only ourselves and Peanut but also the pub as the locus of Pete's life, the bent ex-copper that ran the place and approved of such antics (after the event), and our image of ourselves as adventurous young men. In a straight choice between ego damage and possible death we would choose possible death every time.

The plan as outlined, with deadly serious humorous asides on weather conditions and the possibility of leaves on the track, was to reach 100 m.p.h. on a narrow single-lane road, dead straight except for the bend at the end that could only be taken at 20, max, it was that sharp. The straight was about a mile long and Peanut had done it before, just.

The problem was anchoring up before the bend, said Pete. Peanut had been so keen to go over the ton that he'd left it too late to brake. The car had locked up and spun, miraculously missing two huge chestnut trees and only lightly grazing the hedge.

I got into the back of the car, feeling myself awash with beer. This did not have an anaesthetising effect, instead it seemed to be making my heart beat faster and more loudly than usual. I wedged myself lengthways, half off the seat, then I got right off the seat and wedged myself behind the two fronts. Pete glanced down but said nothing. He knew what I was up to. I got back on the seat and looked longingly at that haven of saftey down in the footwells. But it just wouldn't do. To sit there would be an insult to Peanut and to cast ourselves in a bad light. Pete sat rigid in his seat, without the belt on, of course, because Peanut wasn't wearing his seatbelt. Then Peanut relented and put his seatbelt on, so Pete, very hastily I noted, was able to buckle up too.

We drove down dark, wet, winding lanes, the sky blue and black with moonlit clouds above us. The car began to accelerate.

So that Peanut wouldn't have to look away from the road – brightly lit, it must be said, by Peanut's rack of lights at the front – Pete called out the speed as we went along: 60, 70, 75 . . . 80

. . . it was an old car, but Peanut had dropped a V6 into it and there was no shortage of speed. Pete called out the numbers: 85, 86, 87, 89 . . .

Then I saw the double searching beams behind the hillside, seemingly random, wavering before breaking the crest, then fast down the hillside, heading inexorably to the bend at the end of the back straight.

'There's a car coming,' I said.

No one said anything for just a beat more than normal.

'We'll be all right,' said Peanut, totally flooring it now.

93, 95, 96 . . .

'It always hovers a bit at ninety-six,' continued Peanut, in a cheerful conversational tone . . . 'Ninety-seven.'

'Do you know, I think that fucker's going to beat us to it,' said Peanut, a moment later.

'We're dead then,' I thought. Then I sort of concentrated with my stomach, connecting without words to my luck God. I was drunk and didn't even have my glasses on. I was only visiting Pete for a day and we only came to the pub on the offchance and now death awaited this random series of life choices. What a fool I was, but then had there been any choice?

'Let's do it anyway.'

'Ninety-eight, ninety-nine,' Pete's anxiety now in his voice. 'One hundred!'

Only Peanut was dead calm. Peanut hit the 'Colonel Bogie' horn and its stultifying loudness filled the entire night.

'Shall I see if we can take that corner, lads?' A few seconds of complete horror relished by the humorous Peanut before he dibbed and dabbed the brakes very expertly so we didn't entirely lock up. The other car was waiting the other side of the bend, passive, a family of four in a Princess, late home from some family occasion, perhaps.

'And roightly so that they should wait,' said Peanut, nodding as we passed them.

11.04 a.m.

Dave appears in his Land Rover with the big barbecue. It's a rough and ready model welded up from a section of an oil drum with a metal grill on top and legs made from angle iron, much better than some prissy shop barbecue set up.

I was at school with Dave. Both of us were in the minority of 'bright' kids that went to university, and, like me, Dave has eschewed a conventional career. He prefers to work on his own as a self-employed forester and tree surgeon. Part of it is a desire to work out of doors doing manual labour. He was very ill during his last year at university, contracting a rare kind of stomach disease that the doctors said could be fatal. That was fifteen years ago. Dave noticed he always felt better when he was outdoors and in the woods especially, so that is the work he has always done – at first as a labourer and now in the more conventionally acceptable position of a woodland manager.

When we were at school Dave was smaller than me and not as strong. I'm still a little taller but one look at Dave's arms is enough to convince me, if I needed convincing, that Dave is incredibly strong; much stronger than me. His arms, raw red and sunburnt and scratched, are like great hefty tubes of muscle.

'Where do you get those arms?' I always ask.

'Working,' he always replies.

It's true, his forearms have the well-packed skin-bursting fullness of work arms rather than the fair shapeliness of gym-built arms, but it seems inconceivable that just humping and lifting a few logs could build such monstrous appendages. Especially as most of what Dave does involves a machine of some kind. I look at my own arms, respectable enough, but alongside Dave's my hands look like big useless accessories on the ends of little sticks, like the hands of prisoners kept on starvation rations. Dave's hands have inverted knuckles, a dimple over each knuckle instead of a protrusion. You get the impression that even using an axe to chop Dave down wouldn't work, not unless you took a lot of swings and he wasn't moving. When all men lived in the woods did we all have great hands and arms like Dave? I read somewhere that the ancient bows found to have been used at Agincourt are simply too difficult for modern men to bend, that the ancient archers were not only incredibly strong but they also developed extra bone material on their shoulder blades to cope with the strain. I look at Dave and think how he would easily fit in during any age, even lugging a great bow to fire at the enemy.

Dave is grinning and fondling his little black dog, with one bent-over ear, cradling it in his massive arms. The little thing escaped from the back of the Land Rover and found his way into the kitchen. He really loves that dog.

A lot of people are envious of Dave's outdoor life, though he always puts them right by explaining the tedious aspects of forestry: strimming away at intractable brambles for hours whilst being bitten by horseflies, or operating a sawmill in a freezing downpour.

One particularly envious friend of his, who had money, bought some woodland, but he soon got bored of working it and turned it over to Dave to look after. 'You can't buy a lifestyle,' says Dave. 'You have to earn it.'

Dave's life is a lot less indoors than most. He does things using his strength and skill. And the things he does can be dangerous, that too is an attraction. Somehow all this makes Dave seem more reliable than someone who just does office work, reliable in the really important sense of when the shit hits the fan and no one knows what to do.

When I started this project I surveyed the rights of passage enacted by different primitive peoples around the world. From tribes that hunted the young men (who wore white paint that only faded after a month, if they survived that long they were then warriors) to groups that forced the young to eat strange and revolting food for weeks, to tribes that required a warrior to hunt a wild boar alone (this had, in former times, often been a headtaking tribe) to the West African tribe that force a young man to have spear driven down to the bone of his thigh whilst he smiles all along.

Some of these rites of passage were initiations and used ritualised, rather than real, pain and danger, rather as secret societies in the modern West do. But some of the rites of passage featured some real act of courage or endurance – in one Palestinian tribe the rite of passage was to live by begging for two years, then you were able to come back to the village, get married, start your business and become prosperous.

I was interested in these kinds of rites, rather than the ritual initiation kind, because the latter required you to accept the belief system of the tribe concerned. I was more interested in rites of passage, ROPs I started calling them, that made sense even to disoriented modern men at the beginning of a new century.

Male and Female Energy

My elderly but incredibly youthful friend Eleanor has just reminded me that no book about masculinity would be complete without something on male and female energy. 'You're too intellectual,' she says, implying that the apparent mystery of male and female energy which comes to us without the blessing of science should be accepted despite a lack of proof.

Eleanor believes that men give off a certain energy that women need from time to time, otherwise they become unbalanced. She implies that men also need female energy otherwise they too lose their way. What is male energy, though? Of what is it constituted? I get the vague impression from Eleanor that is an outgoing forceful kind of energy, whereas female energy is a placating, modulating kind of energy. But then again I may just be projecting my own feelings about the subject. Eleanor never tries to explain. 'Just notice it, just feel it,' is what she seems to be saying.

11.25 a.m.

I take the barbecue down to the bottom of the garden and clear some level ground for it to stand on. A stack of wood ready for the walls of the shed I am building will make a handy table. I poke around in the barbecue, trying to get rid of all the ashes from the last fire.

There is something damp and peaceful about this place, overhung by trees and bushes with leaves so many different shades of green. I sometimes sit here on the pile of wood, and instead of starting work just smoke a small cigar and remember how much I used to like similarly shady woodland places when I was a child. There is something calming and secret about such places.

Sitting here doing nothing I notice the wildlife without it noticing me. There are frogs, a hedgehog, a squirrel and a blackbird that is fearless and swoops in low whenever I'm about, as if it's my shamanic companion.

11.35 a.m.

My wife tells me to lock the kitchen door when I come in. I say, why bother? She mentions again the burglar who climbed into next door's garden having come in from the gardens behind. She means 'Low Serotonin Man'. That was several months ago. I'd seen him while I was laying out the foundations for the shed and knew immediately from the bundle he was carrying and the furtive look on his face that he was up to something. After looking intently over a neighbour's fence for a while, he suddenly climbed over. This was into the garden next to ours. He didn't see me until I shouted at him, 'What the fuck are you up to?' He gave me a startled look, scrambled back over the fence, and legged it. Somehow someone running away from you enjoins you to follow them. I was in such a rush I didn't have time to be nervous. Low Serotonin Man looked to me to be in his early twenties, medium height, poor and white. I got on my bike and raced around the block to catch up with him just disappearing into another street. He was walking now and turned back to regard me with polite interest. He'd already ditched the stuff he'd nicked. Before I could speak he had his excuse out, 'I was legging it from someone else who's after me, that's why I ran. When you shouted.'

This lame schoolyard excuse I was having nothing of. I straddled my parked bike and ranted how I'd clocked his face and wouldn't forget and he'd better stay away. Enduring this tirade until that point was reached where I wasn't going to get off my bike and make a citizen's arrest (for what? for trespass?), he started to saunter off, turning when he was a yard or two away: 'And I know where you live too,' he said. At least that's what I think he said, because he was half mumbling and it was one of those comments that are experimental, designed to be retractable if my response were too overwhelmingly negative.

My wife had phoned the police and when they came they subjected me to the usual third degree that honest citizens take as their due. And that was that.

But now my wife is nervous and when I come in late she always calls, 'Is that you?'

The people opposite have a security light which is always on, day and night. Something must have broken but they don't get it fixed.

I never tell my wife about the other times I've seen LSM walking, head held high, through the local shopping centre. Looking like he owned the place.

Weapons

A friend of mine always sleeps with a sheath knife on the bedside table. Another guy always drives with a crook lock under his seat, an old-style one good for whacking people rather than for locking up his steering wheel. These men are doing what men have done for centuries, yet now we consider them weird, possibly dangerous. For some reason the fact of owning a weapon immediately cancels the ability to use it responsibly. The fact of wanting a weapon is taken as a sign of mental instability, even though a weapon is neutral until it is used, and even though we are surrounded by 'weapons'.

In my house I have six razor-sharp kitchen knives in a wooden block, a selection of chisels and screwdrivers (all potentially lethal), two rusty spears presented to me in Indonesia, a parang from Borneo, an adze belonging to my grandfather, a Swedish axe and an air rifle. Even though the air rifle looks like a real gun it is probably far more dangerous as a club than as a rifle.

My house is full of things that could be weapons. None of them is positioned ready to be used against a would-be housebreaker. Perhaps a smart housebreaker would pick up, say, one of the spears and use it on me, though he might be surprised by how easily the rusty point falls off the end. Again, the 'real' weapons in the house, the spear and the gun, turn out to be the most useless. I have never seen a lockknife sharper than the Sabatier meat cleaver that sits on our kitchen table. Why doesn't that bother us? Why are we so suspicious now of having, even demonstrably useless, weapons? Why do we trust the army and the police with their weapons and not ourselves? Is it because of their training, their certificates, their state sanctioned ability to shoot 'if they have sufficient reason'?

When I'm away my wife says she listens to every odd noise the house makes. I say that I'm like that in a new house, but not in a house I've lived in for nearly two years. My wife says if half of what you read is true then you have to be careful.

Paranoia

A few years ago, when I came back from Japan – paradoxically after several years training in martial arts – I was far more paranoid than I am now. Maybe it was a kind of post-traumatic stress disorder brought on by too much aikido.

One night I was at my parents' and I thought I saw someone lifting a bag of sand from the front garden. My parents had building work going on and there was a lot of building material in the front garden. The house was also on a route home from one of the village pubs. Maybe a pissed villager was helping himself.

I shouted, using my loudest, most martial voice, at the shape in the garden and he seemed to freeze. Good, that meant I could clobber him with my wooden bokken, an oak training sword I carried everywhere after my time in Japan. I ran downstairs, grabbed the sword and advanced into the night. My presence activated the security light. In the sudden brilliance I saw that the thief was a piece of flapping plastic there to cover the bags of sand. My parents were now up. They did not make fun of my foolishness, instead they seemed glad that I was there to defend them in any nasty situation, situations, I might add, of extreme rarity in their quiet village.

But look at it from the point of view of the criminal, probably a young man enmeshed in a life devoid of dangerous and difficult challenges. For him crime is fun, crime is enjoyable, as long as you are not the victim. Crime now is synonymous with an inalienable heavy duty masculinity, which is, of course, wildly at variance with the profiles of most criminals. Nevertheless, crime is the ultimate in macho cool.

To break into a house requires nerve. To start a brawl requires guts. To steal a car requires speed, skill, nerve; and the reward is a big thrill. Thinking about the consequences is what civilians do. Real men live and die in the moment.

This is the reality of crime, the essential paradox of our culture. The safer our world becomes, the more masculine and attractive crime will become. As Ernst Junger wrote, 'In the modern period crime is the major form of entertainment.' It is no accident that the profile of most Hollywood stars promotes a youth offender bad boy image before 'acting straightened them out'. No accident that rap stars actually become criminals after they've become stars. Often they grew up quite innocuously, but, once famous as a bad boy rap star, crime provides real evidence of masculinity; after all, however 'bad' your lyrics they are only words.

Die Before You Get Old

According to a survey I read, 75 per cent of the readers of *Red* magazine, which is aimed at women aged thirty and over, do not feel grown up nor do they ever expect to be.

My guess is that a similar number of men would feel the same thing.

By 'grown up' we mean, mainly, I think, like our parents, especially parents who seem conventional and cautious and self-disciplined. People who are in control of themselves. But something in me rebels against the petty tidiness and inflexibility of such lives. In rejecting the whole package, though, we lose out on the benefits of discipline and self-control. We aren't any happier than our parents though we may be cooler. I'm beginning to think happiness becomes elusive when self-discipline is absent.

Consumer culture thrives on impulse buying, greed purchases, fads and fashions, wanting it now. Being childish, in other words. At the same time we're chained to our desks to earn the money to be 'childish' when work ends. The joy we associate with children is absent in such work, and its alcohol-fuelled substitute – 'fun', 'partying', 'the craic' – are pleasurable, perhaps therapeutic, but often mechanical, lacking some essential nutrition for the soul.

A society of children is easier to control than a society of adults. Bruno Bettelheim wrote that the aim of the concentration camps, in the early days, was to reduce each inmate to a mere child, dependent solely on the goodwill of the guards. He theorised that the camps were a tool in subjugating the populace, seeding society with a greater than ever dependence on the state. In the more benign modern era, safety culture, dumbing down, proliferating rules and regulations all play the same role.

Bizarrely, we now have a society where it is 'uncool' to be grown up, where wisdom is often ascribed to infants and idiots savant rather than to the fully grown, where adulthood is a sign of having compromised with something odious, and the punk rock cry of 'Hope I'm dead before I'm thirty' is taken as a sort of hallmark of sincerity of purpose, where being old means you somewhere along the line sold out.

And 'being a man' is about being a grown-up man when we get rid of the distractions. So if most people think they'll never 'grow up' they are saying in effect that they think they'll never be 'men'.

Pro-teenager

My friend Chalky often says, 'I'm a permanent teenager, me. Hope I stay that way.' For him, liking recent pop music is a sign that he is just as he was when he was a teenager. But I have known him since he was ten. And of all my friends he is one of the most 'grown up', the one who most seems like an adult. He is reliable, he gets up early, he doesn't take unnecessary risks, he doesn't drink much or smoke, he doesn't cheat on his wife. He plays badminton . . .

And he was the first of my friends to get seriously grey hair. Grey hair is, after all, the sign *par excellence* of being grown up, of being more than grown up, of being elderly, in fact.

So, Chalky, though he seems 'grown-up' i.e., opinionated, confident and independent and has grey hair, thinks of himself as a teenager.

11.42 a.m.

I'm laying out the meat in a flat dish full of marinading sauce when the phone rings. I pick it up and immediately I am connected to the roaring wayward sound of a mobile being used in a car on the motorway. It's Mario and Jane, early as usual. Is there anything we want them to bring? No, come now, I say, mentally preparing myself for their two boys, aged three and eighteen months, a real handful and set to dominate the party proceedings.

Within minutes a huge people carrier pulls up outside our house. They must have been just around the corner. They spend a long time just hovering around their people carrier when they arrive, as I wait patiently at the door. They are discussing what and who they should bring in and how and in what order. Mario and Jane do a lot of discussing about how they're going to do things. Maybe all parents with more than one child are like this. Somehow there is something exponential about children – two seems about twenty times more work than one rather than the double it should be.

Mario has practically stopped working since they had the kids. He is actually quite famous, in certain circles, being the last of the 'great Spanish Action Painters'. He is about fifty, ebullient and shy by turns, with a round red face and one of those coconut hair styles favoured by endangered tribes. He hasn't a single grey hair, of which he is inordinately proud. Jane, fifteen years his junior, has several in her beautiful wispy blonde locks. I notice, as I always do, that her nose is red and upturned, as if she has a permanent cold. She is weary, as always, but putting a brave face on things. She exclaims to my wife, 'You're hardly fat at all – I was huge!' Meanwhile Mario is already engaged in the three-dimensional football he seems to play all the time with his bouncing curious kids. The children are having a great time, it's the adults who are suffering. It is as if our generation is determined to shoulder all the neglect and selfishness of previous generations, even those as kind and loving as our parents were a teeny bit selfish – they must have been, since why else would we be so fucked up? But we're different, different to all previous generations. No one will bring up kids better than we will.

Jane is tall with very thin wrists and elbows, but they are strong and she sweeps in determined to use our house like a motorway service station for the rest and relaxation of her two, it has to be admitted, adorable infants. When one of them topples a vase I try to voice my exasperation at the takeover humorously. Jane takes no notice but Mario is suddenly alert as a rabbit, solicitous, offering to make the coffee which I offered as they arrived but got distracted from doing as I plunged forward to save the vase. I make the coffee.

Of course there is no milk in the house. Such a lack is somehow indicative of our just-in-time, on the brink of chaos lifestyle. My parents have milk delivered with a special milk carrier outside the front door, with a dial to show how many pints they need. Somehow I can never find the time to even consider having milk delivered, plus I always buy organic these days – and they don't deliver that, I'm pretty sure, though of course I haven't bothered to find out. We don't drink it much and I've forgotten to buy some. I know Jane will want milk and Mario, despite being Spanish, is also a milk-man – all those years in English Art School drinking tea, no doubt.

'We haven't any milk, I'm afraid,' I say, hoping they won't mind too much.

'Oh, it's all right,' sniffs Jane.

But Mario is beaming, he's sensed a way to offset the obligation of their noisy intrusion. 'We can use Marcus's milk, no problem. It's real milk,' he adds, probably for my benefit.

Once, a few years back at my sister's house (she also has kids), I risked a spoon of baby milk in my coffee, but it tasted like vaguely cheesy cardboardy Coffeemate – disgusting. Maybe he's done the same thing.

Mario rushes to the car as I pour hot water on to the freshly ground 'Continental' beans. The cafetière plunger goes down slowly; which I always take to be a sign that it will be good coffee.

The child's teat is removed and one by one we pour milk into our coffee from the bleary plastic feeder bottle.

And there we stand, four adults drinking great coffee in a sunny kitchen on a Saturday morning, congratulating ourselves on just getting by, just coping, just hanging on in there. Drinking the kid's milk in our coffee and surviving.

Remember the Sea

Salesmen may call themselves 'warriors', 'hunters', 'killers', but this is sheer fantasy. The same kind of fantasy that calls clicking a computer 'surfing'.

No one 'surfs' the Net. You surf in the sea.

Hunting doesn't happen in cities, in office blocks or on trading floors. Hunting happens with spears and guns and dogs in wild places.

Male-being and Male-proving

There are some activities that men just like doing: shooting, playing football, building shelves, visiting old battlefields, collecting pen knives, digging tiny irrigation ditches on the beach, tightening bicycle spokes, carving meat, opening champagne bottles so that either the cork flies out or expertly so that hardly a sound is made, messing about in boats, sawing wood – the list of these harmless, low-key activities could be endless. The point is that there doesn't have to be anything competitive about them, men simply enjoy the activity. Of course women, too, can enjoy these things, but mostly they don't. These activities combine pleasure with touching a nerve that tells us that this is men's business. Many men enjoy cooking, but cooking only becomes men's business when it is accompanied by lots of chopping and a sense of expertise. Rustling up a meal simply to feed the troops, expecting and requiring no praise – men aren't good at that. This 'men's business' feeling I call male-being. It gives a pleasurable edge to a pleasurable activity.

Male-proving is different. It often isn't pleasurable, but somehow men get dragged into it. Even winning – proving you're 'better' than the next man – simply leaves a bad taste in the mouth, forcing the realisation that there is someone bigger and stronger around the corner just waiting to have a go. Men like to be competitive, but I'm not really talking about that. Benign, limited, competition can be a male-being activity, full of pleasure. Male-proving is when the 'hook' is in, when what you say or do somehow reflects, or is taken to reflect, on your status as 'a man'. If you feel insecure anything can be seen as a slighting reference to your masculinity. I've found this when talking about martial arts to people who profess to 'hate violence'. They often become verbally abusive and aggressive because they suspect they are being judged as 'less manly' because they can't do a karate chop. Male-proving follows its own bizarre and childish logic; the logic that escalates into road rage, neighbours at war, racial attacks.

Here's the speculation: if life lacks enough male-being opportunities then male-proving becomes more common, more woven into the fabric of life. Men who feel 'unmanned' make a point of showing they won't be pushed around by pushing others around. When male-being opportunities decrease, male-proving creeps into everything and spoils everybody's fun.

Bud Schulberg tells an interesting story about Hemingway. At their first meeting Hemingway kept jabbing his finger in Schulberg's chest and firing off questions about boxing, trying to show who knew the most. Not surprisingly this annoyed Schulberg, who felt impelled by Hemingway's seniority to remain civil whilst being insulted. What could have been male-being (talking amiably about boxing) had been infected with nasty old male-proving.

12.14 p.m.

My brother arrives and with a grunt of acknowledgement, heads out into the back garden to get the 'barbie' going. He is capable of charm and good manners, but feels so relaxed in my company that I am spared their benefits. He is also the king of the barbecue, exercising, in this area, some strange tyranny over the whole family, who have given in to him, and now, whenever there is some outdoor cooking to be done, it is he who has to do it. In some ways we are overkeen to get him out into the garden, anxious to keep him in this role we have found for him and which he seems at least more comfortable with than sitting round the dinner table being pleasant. My brother, four years my junior, sells tank simulators for a living. Not tanks, but the electronic equivalent of them, which actually cost almost as much as a tank, though of course they only 'crash' in hyperspace. You could say my bro' is a vendor of giant highly realistic computer games. It seems a very modern job to be doing and he is very good at it, flying all over the world to sell virtual tanks to actual dictators.

My brother was very happy for me when he heard we were going to have a baby. Over the phone he joshed, 'Feel like a man at last, do you?' He probably realised this sounded rather boorish so he added, 'At least you know you're not shooting blanks.' This is a thought that plays more heavily on him than most. He and his wife, in that desperate English way, never talk about wanting kids but somehow we know they do, yet they've been married five years and there's still no sign. But there was no envy in my brother's voice when I told him, even though, for him, being a man has a lot to do with having children, a view I can't subscribe to.

I look through the french windows and see him methodically

and with his characteristic high efficiency using a 'starter' bag of charcoal to start my organic lumpwood charcoal. 'Starter bags' are full of chemicals and what I most want to *not* have on my barbecued steaks but my bro' is very dismissive of my feeble desire to avoid chemicals and pesticides. In a bizarre kind of machismo he has turned the capacity to endure pollution, additives, junk food into a test of strength. His meat is always British and never organic. I have outwitted him by buying the meat so the only demonstration of his perverse perspective is using the starter bag which he specially brought along, knowing that I would only offer him a newspaper and some matches otherwise. If it can be done using technology my brother prefers it.

Shopping

My brother also surprised me the other day by announcing that he 'loved shopping'. Most men are reluctant to admit things like this. Shopping is women's stuff. But increasingly shopping invades everything. You want to go camping – first you go shopping for all the right kit. You fancy playing tennis – go shopping for a new carbon-fibre racquet. You want to get from A to B, don't walk – go shopping for a bike or, much better, a nice new car. Hypercapitalism serves to turn every human interest into a commercial possibility, into some form of shopping. If this annoys, the only answer is to buy fewer things; the only activities to pursue are ones that eschew things in favour of skills. Certain activities encourage this 'less is more' approach: survival training, martial arts, Japanese crafts, rock climbing without a rope or protection.

Hemingway Paradox

As well as liking shopping and new technology my brother dislikes reading anything except newspapers and the books of Wilbur Smith. I thought he might like Hemingway but he told me the 'stories didn't finish properly'. Unlike my bro', when I was a student, fifteen years ago, I was a devout and careful reader of the works of Hem. For me, then, they seemed like the REAL STORY, truth distilled on to the page: this is how it would be – to be under fire, wounded, gored by a bull or menaced by sharks as you paddled around the Caribbean in a tiny fishing boat.

And Hemingway looked the part too. I now think that is the most important thing about him. There is a brilliant poem by the Russian poet Yevtushenko about an experience in a coffee shop in Stockholm when he sees this character who looks just like Hemingway – same captain's beard, huge shoulders, rugged sweater and pipe. Yevtushenko imagines the Viking ancestors that must have brought forth both this man and, by extension, Hemingway. Then he realises that this man is Hemingway. And he is shocked at just how much like Hemingway, Hemingway looks.

But though he looked like an action man Hemingway was still a writer. According to Martha Gellhorn, his third wife, he only did the macho things when he wasn't writing, and most of the time he was writing. Like most writers he spent most of his time sitting on his backside scribbling and thinking (in Hem's case this included a lot of time standing and writing because of his persistent piles). This activity can't really be called feminine, but it certainly can't be called masculine. It is cerebral, interior, asexual and as far from any conception of masculinity as you can get. The paradox is that Hemingway wanted everyone, including most of all himself, to think that he wasn't a guy who spent all day thinking and scribbling; he wanted people to buy his macho image and the active life it implied.

It is very often true that men who do really macho things don't waste time trying to appear macho – they just are. Members of the SAS are often quiet, well spoken and not very tall. Ranulph Fiennes, one of England's foremost explorers, talks and looks rather like a schoolmaster until you notice the missing fingers on his hands. A former armed robber I met bore a striking resemblance to Renaissance pictures of Christ. The very essence of masculinity lies in performance not in show, in real ability not talk, in doing not sounding off in the pub afterwards. That's the Hemingway Paradox – the more you talk about masculinity the further you get away from it. When I asked an elderly female friend of mine what she thought of the title 'Being a Man' she said, 'It's a good title if a woman was writing the book.' She knew exactly what the problem was – the Hemingway paradox.

I'm not trying to criticise Hemingway. I just think he exemplified to an extreme degree what most men, in the lousy modern world, suffer quite a lot of the time. An absence of the reality of masculinity that they have to compensate for in some way.

It might seem that men don't know what they are doing, since the Paradox binds them by a kind of *omerta*. It makes them sound stupid when they are discussing masculine things. They might even revel in this stupidity because it somehow further vouchsafes their masculinity. This was Aldous Huxley's main criticism of Hemingway, that he equated dumb with tough.

1.00 p.m.

Bang on time, which is a little unusual, Eric has arrived. I have known and liked him since university but still hardly really 'know' him, probably I never will, but lately that has begun to bother me less. All friends are different, not everyone has to be an intimate, or rather intimate in every area of your life. Perhaps they only have to connect to the 'real you' in one area, then it's enough.

Eric is a tall, strongly built man, half Dutch, half Breton. He is popular with women, though somewhat shy; from certain angles he looks like a hirsute Sean Connery. He has a deep voice, measured, and a grip like an iron-bending weightlifter. He is not as strong as huge-armed Dave, yet his handgrasp is ten times stronger.

His hands are big, not huge, but bigger than most hands he encounters and certainly big enough to envelop one's own unsuspecting outstretched paw. The handshake, which must be a habit, perhaps encouraged by his father, a chain-smoking dealer in commercial steel submersibles . . . whatever the reason, Eric has an unusual handshake. It's hardly a functional handshake between friends, unless his aim is to always slightly intimidate, set the agenda. He always smiles like mad as he crushes your hand, grinning like a gap-toothed stoker steaming out of the Waldersee. He wants to make the intimidation illicit, covert.

Or perhaps he wants to bully us, just a little, for fun. Eric is not pompous, aggressive, or even very ambitious. Sometimes he sounds defensive about his meandering life. Then comes the bone-crunching shake, just to let you know he could be boss, if he really tried, if he really wanted to.

Kid's Stuff

Maybe Hemingway would have outcrushed even Eric's handshake. Knowing that someone had a stronger shake would have really irritated Hem, I'm sure. I'm also sure he wouldn't have been ambivalent about handshaking. It would be one of those areas where Papa had laid down the law.

When you're a kid and haven't experience and haven't even read very widely, Hemingway's bluster seems like the only way to tell it. But, gradually, it dawned on me that everyone experiences things in their own way, depending on their preconceptions, beliefs and then, later, what they choose to remember of an event. They certainly either exaggerate or diminish an experience – nothing can ever be transformed into words to perfectly replicate the exactness of an event. And even people from similar backgrounds have different nervous systems, different chemistries, different pain thresholds. I began to see that Hemingway's insistence on 'telling the truth', while an effective polemical stance, a street barker's ploy, had actually not much to do with the truth. And his insisting that he knew the score closed out other viewpoints, the very proliferation of which were serving to lead towards truth. Because truth wasn't in words, in verbal formulae; it lay in further expanding one's horizons, accumulating world views not dismissing them. And Hemingway forced one, along with the sharp clinical prose and romantic settings and adventurous stories, to imbibe his shockingly cynical, depressing and culture-bound world view, and that was that. 'Everything's gone to pot.' 'Things aren't fun any more.' 'The best is all over now.'

And instead of looking inside himself he tried to change the world to improve his mood. Shooting ducks made him happy so he'd go to Venice to shoot ducks. Venice, for Christ's sake! Or hunting lions would make him feel strong so he'd go to Africa and hunt lions. Yet in this desire to change the world in order to improve one's mood there seems to be something undisciplined, childish even.

There's a lack of flexibility in Hemingway's mental, and physical, postures that looks like strength until you have seen the strength of a Japanese aikido master, bending and flexing before everything, waiting for the perfect moment to deliver the killing blow.

More Fear Of Heights

After finishing school I went straight to university without the usual gap year in between. During the summer holidays after my first year, I went climbing in Skye with another student called Boylan. One climb started at the end of a long rock ramp that lifted you high and out over a two- or three-hundred-foot fall. The ramp was as wide as a road, so it seemed ridiculous to rope up while ascending it to the start of the climb. But at the end you had to step off the ramp, on to a big stone scoop, and then on to a wide ledge. For that one moment, when both your feet were in the scoop, which was plenty big enough, and the air fell away beneath you you felt terribly 'exposed' as climbers put it. Exposed means the fact of being high up is really rammed home. Gullies and chimneys, though technically difficult, are not exposed, i.e., not frightening. Exposed really means frightening, but following the tried and trusted method of brave talk preceding brave actions, climbers prefer the euphemism 'exposed'.

Anyway, Boylan and I ambled up this ramp hardly even thinking about the single move at the end, an easy move, but one which, if an error occurred, would result in a two-hundred-foot fall through air, absolutely fatal. And somehow the contrast from the safe ramp to the sudden danger of the foothold was more shocking than during a climb, even a solo climb. It was like climbing out of the window of a skyscraper on a windy day, you know all you have to do is grip on to the window frame, but screaming at the back of your mind is another voice which says, 'What if you let go, by accident, what then?'

Playing in the Risk Zone

When I was climbing, almost all fear (except in unusual situations like 'the scoop' foothold) disappeared in the intricacies of the climb. Even when I was climbing solo, without a rope, the sense of risk was far more diminished than when I was walking around in the normal world. Because you control the risk, it seems less. Climbing, even risky climbing, where a mistake will cost you your life, is more akin to play than danger right up to the moment when disaster strikes. One reason is that a very good climber *is* playing as he climbs. He's enjoying doing something other people find difficult and consequently dangerous. Another reason is that you don't think an accident will happen to you until it does.

Falling

Boylan was tougher than me, of that there was no doubt. Boylan liked wet sleeping bags, leaking and chafing boots, mosquito bites, the cold heavy and persistent rain that can engulf the Island of Skye for weeks on end – all these horrible irritations just made him smile more, laugh uproariously, stride out further and faster. But then Boylan's favourite pastime was cave diving . . . in mud. There is no more dangerous, unpleasant and generally insane hobby than cave diving in mud (unless you count glacier diving), and yet people like Boylan really *love* it.

As we stood by the road in the pouring rain waiting to catch a lift up to Scotland I'd question Boylan about the attractions of going deep underground and seeing nothing, not even your own hand in front of your face. 'It's the buzz,' he'd say. 'Going somewhere that hasn't been explored before.'

Boylan fancied a career teaching outdoor activities at a Kurt Hahn school. Skye had been his idea. When I arrived I realised what he liked best was the continuous rain. Some days it really was too wet to climb so we'd just go walking. Once we came across a hugely deep gorge with a waterfall plunging down its side. Boylan insisted on rigging up a 300-foot rope to abseil down the waterfall 'just for a laugh'. He secured the ropes with a hex nut in a mossy crack, secure enough in an emergency, but hardly bombproof, especially as there was no need to do this mad stunt. I declined and stood at the top, watching his bulky, gesticulating form disappear under pounding tons of icy Scottish water. Typical Boylan, hadn't even tied a stop knot at the end of the rope he was sliding down. When he appeared, half an hour later, he was breathless and soaked to the skin and very happy. He told me, grinning all the while, 'Bloody lucky – the rope ran out only three feet from the bottom.' What if it had been thirty feet? It didn't do to ask uncomfortable questions like that – getting away with it was the main thing.

At this time, the mid-1980s, climbers were just starting to get into body building. There were three tricks that only serious training could enable you to do. One was the full body push-up – flat out, you have to arch up supported by only fingers and toes. The second test was a one-armed pull-up. The third was to hang from a six-inch-wide beam using only the flat grip of the hand and then make your way six feet along that beam without curling your fingers over the top. That was the hardest – even Boylan couldn't do that. But he could do the one-armed pull-up (I tried and failed) – demonstrated in the aluminium cubicle in the gents' loos in the youth hostel. Full body press-ups were the easiest. I could manage two; Boylan did five.

Out on the rock, when it wasn't raining, I got my revenge. Boylan was strong but his ability to move up on microscopic holds wasn't as inventive as mine. Neither was he so flexible. Somehow the competitive nature of things kept getting inappropriately reignited. Waiting for yet another lift to arrive we had a long and pointless argument about odds and betting that ended in a forced and uncomfortable silence.

We decided to move south to Fort William and do some climbing on the Pol Dubh crags on the lower reaches of Ben Nevis. At least the weather would be better than Skye. These were short technical climbs around 5c/6a, which, at that time, was still considered pretty difficult. After one fine day, when I'd had to take over from Boylan to solve a particularly knotty mantelshelf problem and then lead several difficult climbs successfully, I was keen to get back to town for a nice cup of tea before the cafés shut. Boylan was more of a puritan, a nine-to-five climber if ever there was one. He looked at his watch. 'How about one more?' he said. And it was there, just a hint of competition, just a touch of, 'You may be good but I'm the serious one.'

'OK,' I said, 'how about Hodad?' Hodad was 5b and comprised a long upward leading crack that narrowed and narrowed towards the top. Boylan went round the back of the crag to climb up the easy way to get a view from the top. While he was heaving his way up round the back I started to climb, without ropes, fingers jammed in the crack – I'd show him once and for all who was the best. Full of confidence I planned to on-sight solo the whole climb and surprise him at the top.

Soloing is dangerous, but it can be made very much safer by first downclimbing a route, or top-roping the route, or even climbing it first with normal rope protection. There are even ways to protect yourself with a rope while soloing, using a device that pays out the rope from protection points, thus minimising any potential fall. But on-sight soloing, with no ropes, is both the purest and most hazardous of all climbing experiences.

The crack was narrowing and it was difficult but I was solving each problem as I went along. I reached the ledge that divided the climb in two and continued inching my way along the slowly rising crack. It got narrower and narrower and suddenly ran out. I could see the top. Feel it even. But there wasn't a hold to find over its curving lip. I kept retreating back to the last hold, telling myself I wouldn't be able to downclimb what I'd just ascended. I didn't look down. I was too busy. But in my refusal to go back was a kind of failure of flexibility. I was locked. Somehow I had rushed the defences of my mind, convinced myself my luck would hold out as it always did, but trusting in luck is a kind of giving up, a refusal to take the ultimate responsibility.

Slowly my will began to run out. I moved backwards and forwards, backwards and forwards like a trapped rabbit between the last two moves. In my mind I was giving up. Then I felt my fingers slipping from the chalk marked crack. I was trapped but I wasn't fighting. I let go. Falling. Half way down and I braced myself. This was frightening. I was higher than I thought. More than thirty feet. Later I calculated I was in the air for just one and three quarter seconds. Waiting like a kid waiting for punishment. CRACK. My legs shot away from under me as my backside smacked into the ledge. Landing on my arse from thirty feet up, like David Soul at the beginning of *Starsky and Hutch*; there was an immediate pain in my back. But I wasn't unconscious and when I moved my arms and legs they still worked. For a second or two I thought I'd got away with it, maybe just broken my ankle, which was already ballooning up in my boot.

Boylan, it has to be admitted, was superb. He commandered a Mini and had me driven to the hospital – first having organised four climbers into making a stretcher of crossed hands to carry me down the hill.

My ankle wasn't broken; just very severely strained, but my back was fractured in two places. For two and a half months I lay flat on my back in Fort William and watched the Virginia Creeper outside the window turn first red and then finally the wind ripped all the leaves off, leaving it bare. Boylan had to get back to college. He bought me a copy of *Cancer Ward* to read – typical Boylan, but actually it was the perfect book to read because the hero doesn't die.

And even now, writing about it fifteen years later, I've got a wince on my face. And my back starts to ache a little, just to remind me what it was really about.

ROP

Maybe it isn't just a lack of male-being activities that makes men want to 'prove' themselves. Maybe we have a 'need' to prove ourselves, and one purpose of a primitive rite of passage was to deal with this once and for all. After a really difficult and dangerous rite of passage you need never have to prove yourself ever again. Maybe it was a cure for the otherwise ever-present annoyance of male-proving activity.

Primitive rites of passage that featured real difficulties to be surmounted rather than simulated ones can be easily boiled down to one of four challenges, or a combination of two or more of the same four challenges.

The four challenges are:

1) To kill a man or a dangerous beast.
2) To stare down danger coolly and with aplomb, avoiding the 'flinch reaction'.
3) To endure great pain and privation.
4) To achieve great mastery at some rudimentary skill: marksmanship, weapon making, wood carving, wrestling.

The life of these tribes may have been 'boring' in terms of lacking stimulation, but it was rich in the variety of everyday experience because of both the requirements of outdoor living and the necessity of communal life to survive in such outdoor environments. And the rite of passage was certainly far from boring.

The ROP was the most extreme form that everyday experience could take. One might hunt animals regularly, but nobody hunted lions unless they really had to. In headhunting tribes, the head taken could be of an old or infirm person so as not to incite another tribe into fullscale war. Even so there was a risk of war with headtaking, so this ROP is not something that represents everyday life (otherwise they'd always be at war) but rather an extreme version of it.

After the rite of passage men didn't need to prove themselves in any dramatic way again, though the lives of primitive peoples all involve danger and difficulty of a physical kind which keeps men from losing the kind of skills and attitudes so profoundly tested during the ROP.

Learning To Walk

Two and a half months lying flat without moving had not only caused my leg muscles to wither, it had left the soles of my feet incredibly sensitive. Now that I was allowed to stand, I could hardly bear the pressure – even a few minutes was distinctly painful.

We do not think of walking as an activity that requires special adjustments to the usual condition of our bodies. While walking is our normal method of getting around, it too, exacts a price, reminding us that our feet are not hooves, that once the sole was as useful as a hand in swinging through the canopy of the forest. The sole's sensitivity bears witness to its past life as a foot palm, capable of grabbing fruit and branches.

Each day I'd walk a little further. First it was the length of the ward, then into the corridor, then to the end of the corridor. The pain in my soles felt exactly as if I was putting far too much weight on my feet. It felt irresponsible to be walking, as if I was certain to do some sort of damage by putting so much pressure on the feet. Yet I knew I could walk, had walked on these same feet only months before. So, slowly, I relearned walking.

Ego and Justice

In the first few days after the fall I remember having an almost hallucinatory certainty that 'one must do good'. The primacy of doing good starts to unravel in the everyday world where what is 'good' is not so obvious. Nor is it obvious always how to effect a desired 'good' result. The burning desire to do good, whilst useful as a sign of commitment to something outside oneself, is not enough. Lying there reading with my chin propped on my chest I knew the 'do good' feeling was not enough. I needed knowledge first. I needed to know how to tell what was good and what was bad.

I fondly imagined when I started looking for a better, wiser, saner way to live that all 'problems', such as insecurity, lack of confidence, pessimism, would all melt away as I progressively got more and more knowledge. I didn't really understand that this annoying undergrowth of psychological problems had to be dealt with first. There is a saying that one must be egoist in order to then become just. You must do your own thing before you can do things for other people.

Transformations

We admire men that have transformed themselves. All growing up is transformation. Other things being equal we always prefer a grown-up to a child as long as the grown-up isn't a square, a mental case, or, in other words, someone who hasn't really grown up. If the grown-ups aren't fully grown, as is often the case, then we opt for the purity of the child, their energy, but it is second best, really, and anyone who knows kids knows their much vaunted imagination and creativity are like Brion Gysin experiments with cut-ups: innovation by random juxtaposition, interesting but not very useful.

We admire the transformed because we yearn to be transformed ourselves. Who is really satisfied with themselves? Who wouldn't rather make themselves into something better?

After the Fall

Back in university I changed course from engineering to philosophy. I knew now that I wanted to write; all that lying down writing in pencil because a pen ran dry in seconds as I held it upside down. I wrote poems and cogitations into exercise books and thought at the end that I had lived, getting all broken up, just like Hemingway when he was hit by a shell in Italy, almost the same age as me. In some perverse way I thought of this as my rite of passage. I made a big effort never to complain while I was in the hospital, to be a model patient and ask only for pain killers when it was really bad.

Postures

In college I carried a foam camping mat everywhere and lay down to hear lectures. I never sat, only stood or lay, and forced myself to go swimming twice a week to rebuild my back muscles, grown flabby with so much lying down.

Now I was thinking about my posture people used to comment, always favourably.

My thinking changed, new states of mind becoming more habitual. Every change in posture is a shift of the centre of gravity, the centre of your thinking. This new bolt upright, almost spindly posture served me best when I finally did start sitting down. Instead of hunching over books I sat up straight and perused them with grace. No forward lean or caved-in chest. It was as if my personality had been given a second chance to develop.

Secret Histories

A secret history of manhood, of men, manliness and masculinity, might circle such ideas as posture, the stare, the eyes, what isn't said, the looks men give as they walk past each other in the street. But what is this secret history except a history of the secret that all men carry and think, absurdly perhaps, that no one knows?

Each man thinks his own secret is safe, how he became what he is, the hopes and fears he carries around, all that, he thinks is safely hidden. And even if a man should break the silence, think to tell all about his secret life, then all that comes is a few wry tales, sob stories and cautionary yarns and the broken image of himself, all in pieces now and not, after all, what he meant to say. 'It wasn't like that, it wasn't like that at all.' But too late to stop the involuntary drawing of conclusions.

When did I learn to slouch unnoticed into school, stand up and be noticed when I wanted to be chosen for a team, cry like a tiny kid when I broke my arm and lay full of self-pity on the couch at home, face that bully who exploded my nose with a stippled batting glove or lean forward in creaking politeness to ask my first girl for a dance?

We live in bodies we know so little of; they are invisible to us until they break or lead us into calamity. What tiny habits accrue day by day until there we stand, five and thirty years behind us, five and thirty stretched out in front (we dearly hope), pot bellied now, a little stoop, uncomfortable in our bodies, wishing we were someone else when someone else goes past with ease and grace?

If we could know those moments when the die is cast, the flesh becomes stone, our feet take root into clay and wait for the creeping cold, if we could know those moments and take action against the onset of the unwelcome carapace, would we not act?

Those moments, those decisions taken so lightly, they are not noticed – I will be thus, I will stand thus, I will sleep for hours and awake refreshed or force myself to endure pain, the biting cold of bathing in rivers and the winter sea, who knows where such fanciful notions will carry us in life?

Someone speaks highly of one aspect of ourselves, how we did this or carried off that prize, and slowly we turn to become the afterimage of that praise, a hollow reminder of what we almost were. The history of a body, its knocks and peculiarities, its faults and strengths, all that we hardly know and yet that shapes us, shapes that idea we have of ourselves, which again feeds back and shapes us more. That imprint in the brain of our outer form, our movement, that mental tyranny over body and being, of how we move through life, becomes our life, that image of ourselves cast up by accident over the years of growing up, the fingers burnt, the tellings off, the faint encouragement to lie or tell the truth. The picture of ourselves, unknown until we become it in our physicality. The secret always finally does come out since we are doomed to become it – it is our body and the way we move.

The Hemingway Complex

A 'complex', ordinarily understood, is a hang-up, a mental loop we are doomed never to escape from. The 'Hemingway Complex' describes a common condition: a nagging feeling that your life is too soft, not manly enough, hard enough, testing enough. You feel up to a hard life but it just isn't an option in the lousy modern world. Hemingway suffered from the complex all his life. He wasn't relaxed because he knew being a writer is not a macho job. So he compensated with tough-guy sports and promoting a macho image. Now more and more jobs that men do resemble being a writer: sitting for large parts of the day at a desk in front of a screen, tip-tapping away at a buzzing computer.

Men who once were blacksmiths became motor mechanics, who became that guy who replaces the microchip that controls the fuel intake of your car. Work is getting softer, more indoors, less manly.

1.02 p.m.

While flipping steaks my brother has another 'towelhead' story to tell me. He does a lot of business in the Middle East yet he always insists on calling Arabs towelheads. Since I'm married to an Egyptian that's pretty stupid and irritating yet, in the manner of brothers, part of the game is that I never show that I'm irritated. Before he starts one of these stories he always gives me a sly look from under his eyebrows, just to check I won't get really offended, and then he's off. In this story the towelhead driver insists on intoning a verse of the Koran every time he starts the car. They are on the way to the airport in heavy traffic and it becomes apparent that the Peugeot 504 is in desperate need of a service since every time the driver lets the revs drop the engine stalls. Every time it stalls he intones a verse of the Koran before turning the key ('Which verse?' I ask. 'How should I fucking know?' says my brother). It's now getting very close to departure time and he's stalling more and more often. I can just picture my brother fuming and yet knowing enough not to interfere. Finally, just before the airport there is a big pile up which has obviously just happened. Traffic slows to a trickle and there is a lot more stalling. They are late at the airport but luckily the flight is late too. 'You know why?' says my bro'. 'Bloody pilot was probably reciting his verses before switching each engine on!' He seems to have missed the point. 'If the driver had been going any faster you might have been in that pile up too,' I say. My brother just waves his steak spatula dismissively. I persist and remind him of an accident he had a few years ago when he got into a silly duel with a BMW driver in Esher, where he lives. He was driving his Subaru Impreza, a car that looks ordinary but is extremely fast, and he hates being overtaken, even in a 30 m.p.h. zone, which is what happened. In revenge he was aggressively tailgating the beamer when the driver sharply braked at a light just going red. My brother never stops on such occasions and drove into the back of the BMW. I remind him that he confided to me at the time that most of his problems in life have come from trying to 'prove himself'. This time he looks at me and says, 'I never said that!'

Counter-culture Perspective

Oh no! Not more theory! And 'alternative' theory at that. I imagine getting my brother to read this book – phrases like 'counter-culture' really crack him up. Counter-culture to him means combat trousers and begging and mangy dogs, astrology, crop circles, UFOs and Stonehenge (his theory is that it was a prehistoric service station on a four-lane goat track between Woking and Bath), acupuncture, ley lines, dowsing and crystals, dreadlocks, palmistry, Greenpeace and vegetarian food.

But I've got something different in mind. By 'counter-culture' I mean a way of thinking in which learning from experience is an integral part, in which personal transformation is a belief, in which life is seen as a journey, not a destination. If you want UFOs and swimming with dolphins too, that's fine, but it isn't necessary to what I'm talking about.

Modern men who have undergone something similar to one of the four challenges of a primitive rite of passage should be different, shouldn't they? Transfomed and content and without hang-ups? But that isn't always the case. If they have no beliefs concerning its importance as a learning experience in their lives then it remains as an undigested event, a good story, perhaps, but nothing more. The enzyme for digesting such a difficult and dangerous event is the inner orientation loosely defined as counter-culture. This is to distinguish it from the mainstream materialistic culture. The counter-culture puts greater emphasis (though far less than a primitive culture does) on the role of the invisible realm in determining our lives. The belief that happiness is 'caused' by having more things, more relationships, more freedom, more time is the materialist perspective on life. It is identified by its mechanical method of quantifying the unquantifiable, of using methods that work when counting bricks but don't work when accounting for the finer movements of the human soul.

It may be that, in ridding oneself of things, one becomes richer – feeling freer, less 'owned' by the objects in one's care. It has been observed that people who orientate their lives around the experiences they find most meaningful, rather than the most pleasurable, are in the long run the happiest. And as billionaire Dave Geffen put it, 'People who think money makes you happy haven't been rich enough long enough.'

The idea that one's life is a journey and that one can and should be learning all the time is a major feature of the counter-cultural view of life. This learning isn't to get a job, as the mainstream dictates all learning should be, rather it is seen as a reflection of a greater learning which is to find one's place in the grand scheme of things. And a belief that one might have some significance in a world that in all its formal aspects constantly undermines self-worth, requires a belief in the ultimate connectedness of things, ideas of a transcendental purpose to life beyond mere selfish gene swapping; in short, a belief in the invisible and the Absolute.

The mainstream requires only that you believe that life is nasty, brutish and short unless you have Penicillin and Prozac, in which case you should plan for a ripe old age in which to enjoy yourself. Such a view has penetrated even down to rebellious youth – 50 per cent of eighteen- to twenty-four-year-olds recently questioned in the UK claimed they were 'looking forward to their retirement'. The mainstream is geared to encouraging the view that a great life is tantalisingly just around the corner if only you have enough money saved.

Thick Head, Clever Hands

As a student I could never take university seriously. After all the parties and interesting people one met, after the fun, the coffee-fuelled discussions, the girls and the incredible languor of just sitting around in other people's rooms, I sensed I was insulated from real experience, though I wasn't quite sure what form that experience should take other than knowing it wasn't in common rooms and lecture halls. I finished my exams and went to the other extreme, taking a job working on building sites in Birmingham. One foreman, an Irishman getting on in years, could only write enough to sign his name. His chat was none too bright but when he picked up a pick and used it to solve a problem, breaking through a tricky layer of masonry lodged beneath the earth, his hands became quick, sure, able to solve anything. Mine were fumblingly slow on a task like this, however keen and energetic I was. A lifetime working on the buildings had educated his hands, made them intelligent.

Blue Collar

Blue-collar workers don't have to pretend to like the job. The job is for money, there's no hypocrisy about careers and commitment, and when it's six o'clock it's over, you are a free man until eight the next morning.

The best blue-collar work is smashing things up, digging holes with a shining pick, sawing, hammering, using your muscles out of doors, rain or fine, with enough time, but not too much, for tea and a bacon sandwich in a café.

Skilful work is better, but skilful work that you can get paid for often involves machines. Using dangerous noisy machines, like working on the drills eight hours a day, was not for me. Power saws and nailguns, planers and spindle moulders, routers and jointers, all these things complicate the muscular simplicity of blue-collar work.

Working in factories, becoming a machine yourself, is also ranked as blue collar, but for me that kind of job is little better than office work. Every day ought to be different, working at different places, getting about town.

Theory Versus Reality

My ideal job would be doing manual labour of some sort with my friends. We could talk, joke, have a fine time and still get some exercise and do some work. Unfortunately the kind of people I was working with on building sites in Birmingham were not top-drawer construction workers. The *crème de la crème* of builders were all down in London experiencing the greatest boom since the beginning of the seventies, and even in

Birmingham the serious hard hatties would be involved in projects requiring real skill, probably using machines. The work I'd landed was with the council, clearing old sites, putting up security fences, demolishing brick eyesores from previous eras of prosperity. My fellow workers had all been sucked into the scheme as a way of coming off the dole. I, too, had been on the dole, but only for a few months. One member of the team had been drawing benefit for fifteen years, finally his wife had got him this number. The work wasn't too hard, and I did learn how to put in fence poles, but in the end the workshy, humdrum, defeatist atmosphere of the job got to me. Black guys who worked in my team would turn their backs to the road whenever a bus went by – they were ashamed to be seen by their mates to be wearing council workwear. The white workers (there were no Pakistanis or Indians despite their large Birmingham population) were easy going but unambitious – even reading *The Mirror* branded me as an intellectual. I was back to hiding again, just like at school, keeping your ideas to yourself so the hardnuts won't notice you, only coming out with the crudest jokes, farting in the Transit as the highpoint of humour. It wouldn't do.

Confidence

My dreams were always of freedom and the far away countries I liked to read about. As a prelude to freedom, or an inept way of gaining it via the acquisition of a huge pile of cash, I quit downbeat Birmingham and settled in London, imbibing like oxygen the new enterprise culture. I signed up for a new dole scheme that aimed to encourage sparkling new commercial innovations and so embarked on a series of interesting business failures.

The business failures were, broadly speaking, all connected with 'high concept' ideas. 'Batman and Robin Car Cleaning Services' was predicated on the original idea that people would enjoy, and, indeed, pay a premium for having their cars valeted by Batman and Robin. I was going to be dressed as Batman and my friend Lloyd was going to be Robin. The idea emerged because cleaning cars was, apart from driving and putting up fence poles, the only skill I had. Lloyd's only skill was typing, though he didn't fancy being a male member of the typing pool. I assured him I could pass on my valeting skills very quickly, possibly over several pints in the pub. Our simple dream was freedom from the chore of having to sell our physical presence for eight hours a day, but Batman and Robin were not, unfortunately, the solution. The scheme foundered when the landlord refused to allow my phone to be used for a business. Lloyd didn't have a phone so that was the end of it.

Then followed a short lived excursion into homebrewing. In an attempt, worthy I think, to encourage a friend to give up his job and start a business I suggested off the top of my head the manufacture and sale of large teabags filled with oak chippings. These could be dunked in demijohns full of homemade wine to get that added 'oaky' flavour. He wasn't convinced so I decided an example of business acumen was needed. I obtained a sewing machine, net material for the bags, sacks of oak chippings from a carpentry shop and took out costly advertisments in the homebrewing press. Unfortunately homebrewing is a cut-throat field and several similar products easily crushed 'Oake Soakes' as the product was wittily termed.

The next project was the Tube Timer, a handy device that allowed you to measure exactly how long it would take to get from Turnham Green to Highgate. There was talk of Foster's Lager giving away free Tube Timers on New Year's Eve but they decided to give away free Tube tickets instead. The concept behind the Tube Timer was superb, and if it had been computerised it might have worked. Unfortunately the manual version was made of cardboard and resembled an early medieval navigational device for checking star positions. It was vastly complicated and only accurate if the trains ran on time. Any delay required using the 'adjuster', an easily bent slide-rule-type device that responded badly to inaccurate handling. At one sales presentation an eager executive managed to compute a negative value, actually travelling back in time on his hypothetical journey from Tower Hill to Highgate. 'You wish,' said the director, and that was the last we heard from that particular company.

One of my favourites, that almost worked, was 'Gorbachocs – chocolate heads of famous world leaders'. 'Bite off Maggie's nose today.' 'Give it to Reagan in the neck.' A man from a leading chocolate firm in the North West travelled down to London to attend the Gorbachocs presentation. He admired our artwork and our potential advertisement campaign but told us bluntly he hadn't got £100,000 to invest in tooling up for 'heads' that lacked staying power. He was briefly taken with the idea of chocolate medals but 'Bite off a DSO today' somehow didn't have quite the same ring, and he soon gave up returning my calls.

Some ventures never got past the design stage: the cot death aversion cot rocker, the freeze once food indicator freshness roundel, the passive smoking protection kit and the Deerstalker Collective (a chain of shops featuring high quality clothing entirely modelled on that worn by Sherlock Holmes), not forgetting the Buddhist board game – where the only way to win was to lose.

Sometimes I found it hard to conceive that I would ever not be scratching a living in London. I could not see any reasonable escape route without someone handing over that elusive cashpile. I was in such a hurry that I couldn't see the point in saving money slowly, yet you can remain in that kind of hurry for years.

Gradually you use up confidence. You do not notice it at the time, but confidence begins to wane as you redefine your ambitions downwards, take a 'reality check', put on a suit, join everyone else.

1.10 p.m.

Just as the first of the steaks come off the barbecue it starts to rain, heavily enough for everyone, and there are about fifteen people here now, to crowd into the dining room and kitchen. Manfully my brother continues his lonely vigil out by the barbecue, wearing his Barbour car coat and grudgingly accepting a baseball cap to stop his hair from getting soaked. Wine glasses in hand a few of us watch him at work through the window, rain spitting and steaming off the fire. Cleverly he keeps enough steaks going at one time to stop the rain from putting out the coals. He seems to be enjoying himself, in the grim macho way that he enjoys anything, and never once looks towards the window where we are gesticulating and giving him encouraging thumbs-up signs, knowing that this will slightly piss him off. The steaks, when they come, are, as always, delicious.

More Male-proving

My brother does enjoy himself, but he always manages to give off the atmosphere that enjoying yourself (unless you're drunk and therefore not in control and not to be blamed) is a little childish, a little less than grown up. He always dresses up things he enjoys as something else, something useful such as cooking for the family.

But he is also highly competitive, which interferes with his ability to enjoy the things he enjoys doing. If I muscled in on his cooking he wouldn't like it. I know he'd become grumpy.

After some reflection, though, I realise he actually likes being grumpy and pissed off. So if his male-being activity, such as doing the barbecue, should become infected with male-proving (showing me who is the best cook), then he doesn't really mind because it gives him an excuse to be grumpy.

Almost all activities can be subtly altered to have this 'proving' aspect to them, which, of course, gets in the way of simple enjoyment. Even a barbecue can be spoiled by men proving they are better cooks than one another. Spoiled for some men, like me, but not for my brother.

In cultures where the idea of enjoying yourself 'too much' has taken hold as a 'bad thing', people go to considerable lengths to justify their harmless self-pleasuring as something else. In this my brother is entirely in sync with our own 'killjoy' culture. When he goes to a football match it's for corporate entertaining. Even his unfeasibly fast car is justified as a 'business tool'.

It also follows that if harmless self-pleasuring turns out to be rather unpleasant (walking up a wet Welsh mountain springs to mind), then it is also acceptable to the 'too much fun is bad' school.

If doing the things he likes doing also makes him feel vaguely grumpy then my brother feels no guilt at enjoying himself. Because an activity perverted by 'male-proving' actually ceases to be fun; men like my brother can enjoy themselves without the guilt that usually comes with 'enjoying themselves'. He doesn't mind his male-being activities being spoiled somewhat by male-proving; for him it simply means that he is a useful (i.e., miserable) member of society rather than a useless hedonist.

Brain Chemistry and Natural Inheritance

Things used to be much more simple.

For 99 per cent of our time on this planet men have survived by hunting animals and living in small tribes. In the last 1 per cent of our evolutionary history we have been farmers. And in the last 1 per cent of the time we have been farming we have also evolved such non-physical occupations as selling tank simulators. From the evidence of bones discovered from both hunter-gatherer tribes and farming communities we can see that there was a palpable decrease in health as mono-nutrition (rice, wheat, oats) replaced the varied hunter-gatherer diet, and the increased labour of a tedious variety affected bone and muscle health and growth. From all the evidence available the advent of farming resulted in a drop in health. The same happened with industrialisation, with a recovery once modern medicinal knowledge about hygiene began to take effect. But from a physical point of view the modern office male is far inferior a specimen when compared to the burly farmer or the well muscled hunter gatherer. From a physical point of view, if one discounts disease management, becoming modern has been a disaster.

More importantly there is the implication that by living modern interiorised lives we are going against 99.9 per cent of the history of the species. That really doesn't bother some people but it bothers me.

In terms of brain chemistry, the fact that on average most men have ten times as much testosterone as most women, results in a differing requirement for activity. One has to be wary of moving from a single chemical to a suite of behaviours, yet there is enough evidence to suggest that testosterone boosts the need for the overcoming of exterior challenges, be they challenges to status, or, more primitively, challenges to survival.

In Which the Author Admits That He Tried To Conform, But Not Very Hard

I tried to get jobs in advertising and marketing but often, for inexplicable reasons, I turned up late for interviews, often in shirts that had been pre-worn and merely ironed. Such shirts react badly after a hectic journey across town to some overheated office for an interview, and no one ever seemed convinced by my spirited demonstration of the malfuntioning Tube Timer as an excuse for lateness.

Something inside me didn't want to do an office job. This thing inside me sabotaged all efforts to gain a foothold in the respectable world of salaries and mortgages and promotions. I just couldn't believe it was natural to put any effort into getting a job, since I knew that a job was just a twentieth-century con trick, a way of swindling you out of living time in return for cash and praise; cash for things you only needed because you were living in a style dictated by the job you were doing; praise to make up for the lack of cash.

It all seemed so bleeding obvious. So why were so many of my friends getting jobs, starting careers, chasing promotions? Because they wanted to achieve something that the world would applaud, the crummy, plastic-chaired world of personnel and employment agencies, of coffee machines in reception and people on 'hold', of fax machines, and carpets that gave you mild electric shocks, of boardrooms and bored rooms, boredom peeling off the walls like a century's worth of wallpaper, the big windows looking out over the city, the air-conditioner vents, the steaming tedium of all employment. No thanks.

Enterprise Disallowed

My free money from HM Government for being an entrepreneur came to an end after two years. Now I really had to get a job. If I couldn't travel I'd travel as much as I could each day: I could drive, and that settled it. I got a job delivering wine to restaurants. It wasn't much fun but I learned all the quick routes around central London. Then I landed a job with a courier firm, delivering packages in a nippy little diesel van all over the city. I loved it.

Mick's Way

Everyone who worked for Shift It, the courier company, was called Mike, except me and Fat Jackie, the radio controller. This caused confusion, so on joining the company everyone had to assume a new name. The boss was still allowed to be called

Mike, but the top rider was called Mick, the second rider John (his second name), another van driver Mack. An Italian called Michel was forced to use the name Fred, and, as he was often lost, the plaintive cry of 'Fred to base, Fred to base,' was often heard and ignored over the radio. We were supposed to use our number for clarification. I was 02. I kept using it even after the company expanded and it was changed to 04. You can get attached to a number, proud of it even.

Mick and John, whose full false name was Michael John Parker, had both been in prison for causing actual bodily harm and violent assault. Many riders used false licences and only told their real names to people they trusted. With me, the stumpy bullet headed 'John' was always polite, formal even. He reserved a different personality for Mick.

Mick told me: 'I went round John's place. He hangs about with some seriously bad men. They nick bikes for the parts, which they break up and sell. I've seen some hard bastards in my time but, I tell you, I was just not comfortable with those blokes.'

Mick had a broken nose and, on first impression, one of the ugliest faces I'd ever seen. Yet after I had got to know him I thought of him as good looking. He'd been a miner for seven years, quitting Yorkshire and England during the strike, going against his father who'd been a blackleg. Mick had worked as a carpenter for three years in the US. He rode his bike on a US licence.

Mick lived in a well-appointed squat on the edge of a housing estate. He liked to blow money on meals at expensive restaurants like Bibendum or Chez Nico. He'd wear his fancy shirts and affect that classless open friendliness you get when you've lived in the States awhile.

Coming back to the squat with his mate and their girlfriends one night they'd been accosted by rough kids from the estate. 'I told them to chill out and leave us alone but they wouldn't.'

So what did you do? I asked.

'Beat them up,' he said.

When these same kids came round to his house to exact revenge Mick had put on his full face helmet and rushed like a crazed Viking out of the house wielding a baseball bat. Not surprisingly they left him alone after that.

'Why'd you have a baseball bat in the house?' I asked.

'Always have a bat around the place,' advised Mick.

John's Way

John looked like a squat barrel of menace. He'd been inside for a year on remand but had been able to get a friend to terrorise the main witness against him. He and Mick would smoke dope after work on a Friday in a doorway opposite our major clients, a well known estate agents. John had hurt his foot during training with the Paras. He had a son who lived with the estranged mother. He was rebuilding a classic Matchless motorcycle as 'an investment' for his son. He was more animated telling me about all the Rastas he'd scalped with his bowie knife, a fucking vicious thing he showed me once, with a brass knuckleduster guard. 'You can feel that when it goes under your ribs,' he chuckled. He also had a chainmail vest he sometimes wore under his leathers.

John spoke to me in the cunning, careful way I imagined he reserved for those in authority, on the outside, not really trusted. Round the back of the estate agents, smoking dope with Mick, I glimpsed the side of him that had contempt for the likes of me, just the quick look in his eyes, the way that with Mick present he had no need to say the acceptable thing any more. Despite his violence, in which, needless to say, he was always cast as the defender, the attacked, the hard-done-by, he was always basically polite to me but I could tell he had a temper. Little things drivers or pedestrians did made him furiously angry for just a moment. I saw his miserable career as a chain of such moments of losing it, of not being able to control himself, a succession of mere minutes linked together and stretching back to his childhood and defining his years.

2.00 p.m.

The rain has stopped and I get a sudden urge to do some cooking of my own. My brother claims the charcoal is no longer hot enough, but I heap it up in the middle and it's fine.

Standing there in the radiant heat, metal spatula in hand, turning bangers and vegetable kebabs over the hot coals, I am reminded of an uncle, now dead, who owned a sleek thirty-foot sailing yacht. He told me he would take me sailing around Britain with him in this yacht when I was twelve, but by the time I was fifteen I realised he probably wouldn't, despite my incredible excitement at the prospect and despite his full intention of doing the trip when he spoke about it. He just didn't have the time, and deep down perhaps I knew that it would never happen – sailing around Britain with a favourite uncle (he also had a tuned MG which he drove extremely fast) was something that happened in Arthur Ransome, not in boring old modern day Britain. And yet my memory is of him, just a year or two before he died, standing at the barbecue like me, wine glass in hand, cooking up a storm. I think of all the true adventure books he had on his bookshelves. My little adventures are necessary and should not be put off. I'll drink to him, keeping the spirit of adventure alive, passing it on to me despite being unable to do all the things he wanted to do.

The River

I crossed the Thames by bridge three of four times a day while driving my van. It was a vital source of nutrition for me, this river crossing. At that stage in my life, driving the van and writing books which kept getting filed away, I needed all the extra inspirational river energy I could get. So every time I crossed the river I used to look at it carefully and almost drink in everything I saw, refreshing myself with its natural grandeur. A by-product of all my observation was that I had seen the Thames in every condition, from full flood to the veritable trickle it becomes around low tide.

At a noisy party of people doing well, in one of the first yuppie flats being built in Bermondsey, just in front of Butler's Wharf and overlooking the Thames, I got into a discussion about the river. At that moment, from the yuppie balcony, a cold wind blowing and the sound of the tide washing at a great rate past the Tower Bridge pilings, the river looked enormous and wide and dangerously fast flowing. I explained that at low tide it would look meek and shallow, as if the plug had been pulled out. 'You could cross it on a homemade raft, no problem.'

This was not believed. It really got people's goat that I could downplay the obvious danger of the tidal Thames. An assertion that something isn't dangerous, but just looks it, always meets extra fierce rebuttal from people who imagine the world to be more dangerous than it really is. I needed cash and, instead of arguing, I found it easy, for the first time in my life, to make several large bets with friends and wealthy acquaintances. I bet that I could cross the Thames – to start beneath Tower Bridge and to land just beneath the yuppie flat – on a raft made from driftwood, or what I could carry to the Thames in two hands.

My raft needed to be simple. Two car inner tubes lashed together in the middle to make a figure eight. Two pieces of wood lashed to the outer edges of the tubes with an orange box upturned on top as a seat. Almost any piece of wood, even thin sticks, can serve as a paddle. I was taking no chances and fitted narrow plywood blades to the ends of two short sticks that could be bolted together to make one long kayak-type paddle. I was no carpenter, but I knew what I wanted and I knew how to bodge with the right tools. The whole kit, when deflated, fitted into the orange box, which I fitted with straps to make a kind of backpack.

At the river, on the day of the challenge, everything looked hopeless. The Thames was in full flood and there were police everywhere. Everywhere. This fuelled my Charles-Bronson-steals-a-boat-in-*The-Great-Escape* fantasy, but made the sudden loss of several hundred quid I didn't have look sickeningly likely.

The police were marshalling a 'fun run' along the Thames towpath. I cursed all fun runners. Fun running was strictly for losers. Crossing rivers on bits of wood was the real thing. Fuck the fun run.

But the river in flood, that was my fault. I'd miscalculated from the tidetable. I could call it off, but then I'd lose the money.

My friends wanted me to succeed. Stuff like this was better than television. They wanted to help.

This was the problem: me and the inflated tubes and wood needed to be hoisted over a high metal gate under Tower Bridge. There are only six legal boat launching places on the Thames and this wasn't one of them. An attractive policewoman and a surly looking bearded policeman stood in front of the gate. A little way off, another copper, seemingly bored, looked over the wall at the river and the foreshore.

The plan: distract the first two cops, boost me over the gate, distract the cop watching the beach so that I could scuttle for cover under the pier next to the bridge. Hope that I had enough time to get clear before the balloon went up. We were all using language like this by now: World War 2 lingo ideally suited to such an escapade.

My friend Mike returned to his car, and, ignoring the pedestrians only sign, drove it slowly through the milling crowds towards the gate. He parked twenty yards away, opened his bonnet and started to fiddle with the engine. The gate cops approached Mike.

I knew the routine from *The Colditz Story*: Pierre Lebrun, first 'home run' from Colditz, arguably the most daring, was boosted over the ten-foot barbed wire fence by two friends, each holding a foot. Back at the river, with the police away, the inflated tubes and bits of wood were lobbed over. Quick check on Mike – he was gesticulating like an Italian while the cops were pointing. No time to plan how to land: I ran at my two friends, put one foot then another in the suddenly proffered hand hoist, and was boosted to the top of the gate, the upward momentum allowing me to swing my whole body over leaving me snagged on my sweater at the top. The bonnet of the car was now down. The cops were turning away. But they didn't see me. They turned back to Mike, who must have said something. I got clear of the gate and dropped to the ground.

With my back to a stone pillar I was directly beneath the policeman looking out over the river. I would have to cross his field of view to carry the raft bits the twenty yards or so to the cover of the pier.

From my position I couldn't see him so a warning whistle (the opening bars of the *Dambusters* theme) had been agreed. Now I just had to wait, and trust, that the whistle would signify enough time to cross the deadground. I lit a cigarette, knowing the breeze would disperse the smoke. Lieutenant Commander W. L. Billie Stephens chain-smoked during a Colditz break and Howard 'Hank' Wardle had even absentmindedly left his pipe at the top of a moat when he escaped. Smoking was all part of the escape drama.

Soon it was time for another cigarette and then another. I thought I'd been forgotten, or perhaps hadn't heard the whistle. I had to trust. Remember that bit in *The Great Escape* when the idiot doesn't wait for Steve McQueen's signal as he's about to break out of the tunnel? – he screwed the whole thing up.

Then far along the river shore I saw someone in chest waders coming towards me, stepping carefully through the mud. He was wearing a blue sweater. Shit. River police.

I was in a torment of waiting as the man toiled his way along the bank. Then the whistle, which I'm sure was *633 Squadron* rather than the *Dambusters*, but who cares, I was away with my bundle of bits, scarpering towards the cover of the huge wooden pier. The river cop continued his slow advance. In this stinky sea-weedy place I calmed myself, deliberately being methodical as I put the boat together. I had timed myself and knew I could manage it in under two and a half minutes. No need to hurry now. No need to panic.

At that point the cop in the blue sweater waved to me. He was too far away to shout. His wave looked friendly enough. A moment's hesitation, middle-class programming that the police were our friends. Fatal. Without bolting the paddles together I launched the curious raft between the massive square section pilings that held the pier up some thirty feet above me. The water lapped up blackly between the weed-covered pilings and the heavy connecting crosspieces. I hoped the raft would stand up to heavy water. I'd tested the thing quite extensively, but in the relative calm of a friend's swimming pool. This would have been fine for a calm Thames, but I could not wait for that.

Four minutes to cross something like three hundred metres of water. If I was lucky and the current didn't take me.

Wedged against the last piling I bolted the paddles together and then with a massive adrenaline-charged surge I was out from under the pier and paddling for the other side.

I aimed far higher than the beach to offset against the current. Huge reserves of nervous energy caused me to paddle like a man possessed. Despite all the cigarettes I'd smoked I was not tiring. Think *The Tunnel, The Escape Club, The Jungle is Neutral*. Think Mad Mike Sinclair making his final fatal run from the exercise park, Jock Baillie and the Warburg Wirejob – twenty-two men out in under two minutes using improvised storming ladders, P.R. Reid running the last mile to the Swiss border – always run to the border, a running man doesn't stop when challenged. Think *Wooden Horse, Saturday at MI 9, Courage is the Password, Ice Cold in Alex, Flight of the Phoenix*.

Half way across and I began to allow myself the thought that I might succeed. I checked for the river police. There was no sign of them. The fierce current was at last slackening. I risked a glance up to Tower Bridge. My friends who stood to lose money were waving. The beach was approaching fast through the small wavelets of the river. The sun was shining, had been all the time, only now I could notice it. I secured my trusty raft to a metal ladder in the embankment wall and climbed up to the top. Everyone was amazingly cheered by the event, even though they had lost money, fifty pounds per person. It was the best thing I did all year.

Male Attributes and the Rite Of Passage

What do men admire in other men? Who commands their unalloyed approbation? The cocksman? The millionaire? The man 'at peace with himself'? The man with a hundred children and twenty wives? The man with no children who has conquered both the North Pole and the South Pole tugging his victuals on a sled made of fibreglass?

Of course class and culture have to fit in somewhere – in some groups a bouncer is a respected figure; in others a laughable bully. I wondered, though, if I got extreme enough, could I find something that would illuminate the whole subject of being a man?

In keeping with a notion I had when starting this book that 'being a man is not just about football and shagging' I was wary of including the sexually expert or the merely athletic in any pantheon. In Japan I'd met a man who'd slept with three hundred women. A new one each week, steadily, nothing too fancy, in fact he almost seemed a little bored by the routine of it all. What if he'd slept with six hundred? Or six thousand? Sheer numbers meant nothing. It was his skill at hunting and succeeding with women that men envied.

Great footballers are also envied and yet I knew this wasn't important. Even small kids can be brilliant at football, so like a lot of sport it is more of a return to the joys of childhood than a defining test of manhood. What I was looking for were those experiences that defined the furthest extent of being a man, the four corners of the map, the four extremes that allowed access to a millennia-old male experience. Something that connected us to our ancestors.

I remember the first time I met soldiers who had actually killed people. Almost against your will you can't stop thinking there must be something different about them, that the contents of their consciousness must be subtly altered in some way. It isn't an admirable thing but there is something macabrely impressive about it. Even impressive seems the wrong word. But if I met a woman who had killed I wouldn't get caught like this, I'd immediately categorise her action as unnatural, vaguely repulsive . . .

Now this reads like very dodgy ground to be treading and yet what I'm trying to explore seems to require it. Perhaps it is safer to suggest that being a man is about 'not killing' even though you may be able to. Obviously restraining a homicidal urge is far preferable to murder. But the ability must be there, that's where the dodginess comes in. To own up to the ability to kill isn't something most people feel comfortable admitting. It may be a skill men want to have, but not if it (as some imagine it may) turns you into a psycho in the process.

Pain and privation, too, was another badge of honour, even if it was tinged with extreme tedium like that experienced by the poor souls kidnapped and chained to fridges in the Lebanon for five years. What fortitude they must have had, what balls, what *cojones*, as Hemingway would have said.

Avoiding the flinch reaction is another absolutely integral attribute of the admired male. In hypertrophic form it features as unwillingness to look away when someone catches your eye. As Low Serotonin Males do battle with who can outstare whom as they parade down the high street, the more admirable version of avoiding the 'flinch reaction' is in the boxer who stands his ground, the hunter who spears the lion rather than turning tail and fleeing.

Finally, the skills I admired in other men were those that seemed hard won and required great manual dexterity. They were skills connected with life rather than sport, which always seemed like an enjoyable substitute for higher grade 'life' experience.

I admired a man who made marvellous violins, another who could get a bullseye at 600 yards with a 303 rifle, an expert flamenco guitarist, martial arts teachers (even when they had never 'tested' their skills in fights), a man who made long bows from Italian yew trees he imported himself, a friend's father who was a master cabinet maker, a man who taught himself how to draw a sword perfectly from its scabbard (harder than you might think not to cut yourself). It all sounds somewhat arbitrary, except in all these things I saw a mastery that had taken a great deal of work in order to effect a suspected inner transformation.

Even though the argument was circular (I wanted something that connected us to the past – I found it in modern variations of ancient rites) I found I now had, through the extremity of the the four challenges of the primitive rite of passage, a new way of looking at how male-being could have some edge. It appeared that the closer any male-being activity approached one of the four challenges, the more 'male' it seemed, the more it satisfied some deep need in men.

Das Boot

Somehow I knew the river was the key. Follow it down to the sea and then escape across the waves. Building rafts was all very well but what I needed was a boat. Correction: The Boat. In the *Loot* small ads I'd seen it advertised. Cost: £300; value: priceless. I knew I would buy it the moment I read the ad though I had in fact very little money and usually spent everything I earned. The boat was my escape route planned, my escape fantasy hatched, my potential escape made possible, my escape full stop. A twenty-four-foot sloop, clinker-built with gaps between the planks big enough to wedge your finger in, beautiful lines, an engine that didn't work and, most of all, NOT IN THE WATER. Of course I bought it.

I told my sceptical friends that I was simply 'doing it up' to make a fast buck. No one believed me.

My 'boat' was not in the water for the very good reason that it would sink to the bottom if anyone were so foolish as to try to launch it. Clinker-built boats, or lapstrake, as they are also called, dry out and open up on land. The overlapping planks need moisture to tighten up again and become watertight. If a clinker boat has been too long out of the water then it may never shrink back to almost waterproof condition. It will always be a very leaky old tub.

What had I glimpsed rafting across the Thames? A sort of freedom that I did not know about before, the freedom you feel doing what you want to do on a day when everyone else is being 'normal', doing work for a wage or a salary or exercising their right to leisure. It is a combination of the pleasure of bunking off and fierce pride in the sacrifices made to get to that position. You are doing what you want to be doing. If given a million pounds you wouldn't suddenly give up, you'd continue. It is the discovery that life should be organised around what you want to do rather than fitting in to life's humdrum demands.

The boat was freedom and escape and a promise of adventure. Everyone must chase danger, or the uncertain, the small adventure once or twice in life before the onset of crippling old age. Everyone has a duty to feel they have lived.

I can remember the thrill when I discovered that small boat skippers need NO qualifications at all before setting out to sail the world. Unlike cars and planes, boats belong to the free age before paper started to smother everything. Nor did you, technically speaking, need a passport, though of course it would be somewhat inconvenient without one.

The boat was my siren song, calling to me from the old boatyard, nestling between the knackered ketch with a broken mast and the six-man hovercraft on rotting skirts. The boat, which when painted was as sleek as a wagtail, as pretty, and leaky, a boat as you could ever desire.

Big Boys' Toys

One of the constant refrains of my childhood had been 'when you're a bit older'. Can I go walking in Scotland? 'When you're a bit older.' Can I go hang gliding? 'When you're a bit older.' The phrase stuck, and came to symbolise a whole area of endeavour that people, always older than myself, would engage in. Only today someone rang up about a televison idea featuring 'young writers'. 'You qualify,' the director said. 'But they'd prefer people in their twenties.' Shit. All those years waiting to be a bit older, and now I was nearly too old, would be in a few years.

The Youth Trap

If a) certain things can only be done 'when you're a bit older' and b) you think you'll never grow up and c) still feel the same as you've always felt, then it follows, as night the day, that there will be areas of activity you will always delimit yourself from. Things you'd never consider you 'could do'. Owning and sailing the boat was just such an area for me. Owning boats was what grown-ups did, not kids like me. Not that I thought of myself as a 'kid' exactly, just 'not grown-up'.

One Hot Summer

As the summer disappeared it became clearer, weekend by weekend, that the boat was not going to sail that year. I'm not sure I ever acknowledged this to myself, but I must have known. Instead, I diverted myself wholeheartedly into repair of the engine. In part, this was due to my acquaintance with Captain Knowall. The Captain was not a seafaring man; in fact, the plywood cruiser he was restoring two boats down from mine was his first boat. Like me he disguised his sealust as an unlikely excursion into venture capital. He planned 'to do his boat up' (landlubbers imagine you can 'do a boat up' in the same way as a house. Your first boat teaches you how completely wrong this idea is), sell it for a handsome profit, buy another, larger boat and set sail for Portugal, where he planned to settle to write film scripts. The Captain had already had one film script produced by a Danish film producer who was a great friend. The script he was working on when he wasn't doing his boat up seemed both mysterious and audacious, the plot like a combination of *Dorian Gray* and the Italian horror film *Susperia*. It was a real story, which was so unlike my own literary offerings that I was impressed. The Captain seemed to be at the coalface of wordsmithery and not the effeminate rose gardens I inhabited.

He was a small man with a lip moustache, pruned back into a continuous line above his mouth. He looked somewhat harrassed and fortyish – he told me he'd been running a business restoring old Jags, but then he'd taken off in an old navy bus and spent two years 'running up and down hills'. That had cured his stomach. 'I had terrible guts before that,' he explained. 'All the stress.' He smoked roll ups as thin as a diary pencil, Old Holborn in the foil packets.

Two ten-year-old boys attended him. They were the son and friend of the son of the woman he was seeing at the time, a friendly, passive, quiet woman with enormous, poorly suspended breasts. The woman smiled in a self-deprecating way and poured out tea for the Captain. The boys, who were called, and called themselves, the Chief Engineer and the First Mate, came on the hour and every hour to the Captain, one with his papers and one with his baccy. 'No more than one an hour for me,' he said. When I invited him for a drink at the pub he looked serious, almost as if he hoped he would convert me and my thirsty friends by saying, 'I find drinking slows me down.' When you're in your twenties words like that have no meaning at all.

The Captain didn't know about boats but he did know about engines. It was he who encouraged me to 'rip it out and have a look', meaning the engine. I was understandably nervous about doing this. My knowledge of engines was limited and theoretical, my only tinkering done years before on a moped that ran once and then died for ever. I had confidence that I might remove the engine; that I would successfully take it apart and then put it back together again I had very grave doubts.

The Captain was brisk and to the point; he told me it could be a disaster if the engine was rusty inside and I didn't know. He lent me his professional set of Snap-on wrenches. The engine was coming out.

It could be said that the engine, possessing a kind of life, has replaced the horse and the dog in the line of man's immemorial servants. Perhaps the love of engines is also to do with power, being a master of a source of power? Perhaps. All I know is that I, too, felt strangely excited, almost as if I were performing my first faltering steps as a surgeon, when the single cylinder marine engine was finally wrenched out of the bilges and into broad daylight.

It was a very simple engine – one cylinder, one spark plug, petrol driven with a heavy flywheel and a rope pull for starting. Opening it up, glimpsing its deepest glimmering secrets – the polished top of the cylinder, the gears in the pockets of grease – was like diving for treasure. Would there be jewels or dirt in the chest when the lid was forced open? The Captain looked in from time to time, giving things a whack with a hammer now and again – the universal solution to innumerable mechanical problems. He was surprised that everything was in such good order. The sticky gearbox was unstuck, bearings re-greased, gaskets replaced.

The most baffling part of any engine, for the amateur, is the electrics. Sometimes just unplugging all leads, clipping and unclipping fuses, and cleaning plugs will be enough to fix things. With my engine more was required. The Captain passed on the invaluable advice that the capacitor (or condenser as it used to be called) needed to be replaced. I had long passed the point where, if no one had been helping me, I would have given up. But in replacing the capacitor I damaged a crucial part of the plate where it should be fixed. Now I really was going to give up, but, driving aimlessly through the Suffolk wetlands, I came across, by some miracle, a garage run by a man with a proper workshop still open at five on a dark autumn evening. With a few minutes' crackly blue arc light from his welder my capacitor plate was fixed.

The Captain's Comeuppance

All the time while Captain Knowall was providing a helpful word, an invaluable spanner or monster-sized monkey wrench and regular cups of tea, he was doing his own boat up. Being older and more experienced in the world he understood the absolutely essential requirement of getting the boat in the water ASAP. He knew this but he was also a proud, perhaps even arrogant, man, his pencil moustache bristling when the old hands in the boatyard told him what he ought to do next. Oddly, they never told me, even though I would have welcomed such attentions. The Captain used roof tar on the bottom of his boat rather than anti-fouling ('It's what Nelson used, after all,' he pointed out) and masonry paint rather than yacht paint on his deck ('same stuff only cheaper'). I sympathised with his courageous spurning of overpriced chandlery supplies – he even managed to wangle trade discounts at the building supplies shop he frequented – but I knew he had gone too far when he chucked all the pigs of iron out of his bilges and announced, 'Why do I need ballast?'

His boat had been a bilge keel motorsailer and he intended to use it solely under motor power. The ballast was absolutely necessary in a sail boat, to provide something to counter the side thrust of the sails. In a motor boat there was not the same necessity, though all the 'old hands' shook their heads when they saw him emptying all the old bits of iron on to the ground where his boat stood.

The day the Captain's boat was launched, high out of the sky with, I thought, rather a malicious smack into the water from the casual crane operator, it sat unusually high, like a bath toy or a boat still sitting on dry land. The Captain started the engine, jammed it into gear and shot like a rocket into the opposing line of moored boats, hopelessly entangling himself in yards and sheets and mooring ropes. At day's end, over a rueful mug of tea, he admitted the speed had shocked him – the engine and gearing had been designed to shift the heavy ballasted boat not the superlight piece of driftwood the Captain had constructed.

The more serious aspect of deballasting was not apparent until the next morning. The iron weights had counteracted upward pressure over the whole surface of the boat's bottom. With no ballast the pressure increased in the middle of the plywood sheets in contact with the water. Forced upwards they opened up at the edges, letting in water. By morning the Captain's boat had sunk.

At low tide we were able to recover the boat, pumping it dry and moving it to a mud berth which would keep it above water, even if it filled to the brim. The Captain quickly regained his hold on the situation. Later that day I found him typing away at his new script on a computer he'd converted to run off 12 volts, surrounded by the unmistakable muddy one-colour effect that immersion in river water has on all objects. 'Give us a hand and we'll put the ballast back in,' he said.

New Life For Old

The Captain was not there on that last day when I finally had every last piece of the engine bolted back together with the required three mysterious screws left over (never important). I was beginning to learn the secret of mechanical mastery – just tinker and keep trying and if that doesn't work hit it with a hammer.

It was almost dark. I hefted the battery out of my car and connected it to the starter motor, trusting that over the rope pull. I turned the key and the whole thing rattled, gouts of smoke spluttering out of the exhaust, and then it started, the engine ran. Smoothly, without stopping, until I reluctantly had to. I felt as if I had brought life into this world. That something extra, beyond just the parts and the knowledge was involved. I felt, in fact, that the engine wanted to work, had an instinct to work, was with me on that one. Bizarre though it may seem I really felt the thing was alive.

The Great Escape

Getting the engine to go was the only thing I could take away from my boating summer. But there was something else, now I think about it: sipping from a mug of tea whilst up 'on deck', solidly fixed to dry land but looking out over the estuary. In such moments of idyllic repose all the answers seemed already there, hanging like the gulls, motionless in the air against the breeze. It was simply a question of being calm enough to see them. In these moods I could see my future stretching far ahead, but experienced almost instantaneously, so without that dread feeling of having to wait. I knew I would have to leave my current life, that was for sure, that was the message of the tiny sails of the boats far distant, making it over the bar and out towards the open sea.

2.35 p.m.

Eric has just left and I was ready this time for the megashake. Having bent my hand slightly in preparation his fingers slid around mine and I avoided the crunch.

The handshake is one of our oldest gestures. Used to signify friendship and peace, no sword in the hand, it gradually replaced bowing and courtesying as a more egalitarian type of greeting. In Japan the handshake has yet to replace the bowing, but in the rest of the world it has triumphed over genuflection and kowtowing to each other. One theory has it that handshaking existed as a greeting in Europe before the rise and spread of more hierarchical greetings. Then a general mood of egalitarianism, spearheaded by Puritans and Quakers, brought the handshake back again.

Quintessentially, then, the handshake is a greeting between equals, or, at the moment of greeting, there is a presumption of equality, friendship, goodwill. The hard handshake, then, can be seen as an attempt to smuggle some hierarchy into this brotherly gesture. When Eric crushes our hands he is saying: I am stronger than you. Maybe even: so don't mess with me. All acts of aggression can be recast as pre-emptive strikes, a version of defensiveness. Eric, by squeezing paws hard, is sending a warning that he is not to be messed with. Eric is a big guy. Few people would want to mess with him anyway. I think he squeezes hands hard because he likes it, he can, and he wants to assert himself in a socially acceptable way.

Handshaking and the shaking hand come together when the handshake is used to divine the mettle of the man. A sweaty shake, a hot palm, a limp lettuce grip, or even a hand that is shaking are all a black mark, of sometimes crucial importance.

Couldn't that strong grip also mean, 'You're in safe hands

now'? Just as Eric's father wants people to feel they are in safe hands when they buy one of his expensive steel submersibles.

2.45 p.m.

You couldn't find a stronger difference in handshake than between Eric and John, who has also just left. John's shake is hardly there, less a limp lettuce than a brief wipe with something as soft as chamois leather. But John is no wimp.

Earlier this summer, I invited him to practise a little archery in my long thin back garden. It was a lovely warm early summer day and the big round target, made of artificial straw, with a roundel on the front, stood at the far end of the lawn in front of the high panelled fence.

Before we started, John examined the bow, a nice wooden recurve I picked up cheaply from the small ads, and agreed that it was a nice-looking bow. John speaks carefully, measuring his words. He spends a lot of time on his own, running a one-man building company, and when we meet he likes to chat, illuminating me with the things he's been thinking about recently. Only people who spend time on their own actually say things like, 'I've been thinking about this recently.' As well as being original John is careful with money, and time; always combining several tasks in one trip. For example today he has also been into town to pick up a new band-saw blade, which is why he chose today to drop by.

He pulls the bow back and his rather flat chest seems to collapse a little, as if the bow is bending him. His face looks oddly determined and not at all put off by the uninspiring figure he cuts.

I mentioned earlier that I have known John since he and I were both eleven years old. But knowing someone twenty-four years doesn't add that much. It means, I suppose, that you are less likely to be surprised by what the person does. And you are more likely to forgive them after some transgression which has allowed a certain *froideur* to creep into the relationship, or, if like me, you have simply failed to keep in touch.

Documenting friendships is really a very fascinating business. Because now, when I look back on it, it seems very trivial that I should have anything but extremely relaxed and genial feelings towards John, seeing that we have remained pretty good friends for over two thirds of our lives, for over twenty years.

But, twenty years on, unless you make a decision to bring no baggage, no past remembered slight, no ancient history, no imagined insult, then the chances are there will be something there, some kind of gunk by association, triggered when one says or does something. And now, twenty years on, we don't speak our minds as we used to, nor forget as fast the slights, real or imagined.

Part of the problem is that people want relationships to stay the same, or improve in their direction. No one wants their position worsened, accorded less attention, less air time, less 'respect', less interest.

It seems that as we get older our capacity to fall under someone else's sway is diminished. We are less easily hypnotised. But in our efforts to resist others we are left fearing domination by others. And this fear brings out the worst in most people, short-circuiting their creative qualities.

Back to archery. John takes five shots. We slowly walk up and inspect the target, count up his score. Then I take five shots.

John makes several remarks about 'never having fired a proper bow before' and this being his 'first time doing archery'. This is to cover any failure. I am suitably disarmed and prepare to shoot without too much aiming so as to even things up. Though John works outdoors and is pretty strong, this is his first time and this predisposes me more generously towards him. I give him the best arrows. I don't want John to think I've just got him there to give him a sound and humiliating drubbing.

But even after the first round, John is ahead. He starts to make cautious remarks about the bow, how 'it's intuitive, the aiming'.

Slowly I fall behind in the points. Goddam it, I've spent months using this damn bow each weekend, surely I should be able to pull all the stops out?

Now I casually start to use John's arrows – but there is no noticeable improvement. John begins to make self-deprecating remarks. Actually, I'd prefer him to boast, then it would be out in the open.

When he misses I'm secretly pleased. When I'm aiming I feel real pressure to hit the target. It's palpable. 'Tense stuff,' says John. Which is about as close as we can get to it.

Aiming air rifles as a kid I felt all the same emotions. I've been sharing archery all summer with all kinds of people who beat me or lose to me, but no one has evoked so strongly the bad smell of childish competition. These friends I've known a long time – why should it matter that I still win? When it matters not at all with new friends; in fact, I'd be happy that they beat me.

One aspect is the pretending it's not going on, the so-English self-deprecation as a direct substitute for boasting. But even when I boast that I'm going to wipe the floor with someone it sounds hollow and rings slightly forced if they don't respond in fashion, play along at this game.

Competition arises, the 'bad smell' of men 'proving' themselves, comes about when one party projects an image on to the other, an image that is felt to be false. One could verbally assault this false image, but things are rarely that out in the open. The competition is a way 'to show them'.

But then John is quite cunning. He always urges me into presenting myself in the best light, the more experienced one, the better trained. And then he is able to come from his meek position and overtake me.

Here we both are, no longer kids, and still worrying over our basic archery skills. I talk about false images and projecting but, pushing it further, why should I worry about a 'false image'? You can't control the thoughts of the world. Of course I should just let it be, let it wash over me. A final thought, though: if we turn out to be crap doesn't that mean we would have died out in Stone Age times?

Shift It

I needed a challenge and I needed results. I was twenty-five, driving a van four or five days a week and calling myself a writer. But my writing had not been good enough to show anyone, I believed, so I remained a very unknown writer. On one occasion I read out a novel to two friends over a couple of nights in front a roaring fire in a cottage in Oxfordshire. On both nights snores greeted my precious work in progress. It might have been the good dinner, or the warmth of the fire, the effect of the wine, my reading voice . . . whatever the exact proportions of the ingredients, the combination was a soporific more successful than sleeping pills. I was more careful about displaying my efforts before I was ready after that.

Things were not going so well at the van company either. The familiar sarcastic ring of 'Shift It? More like Forget It!' was directed at me more and more as I shaved schedules to get extra hours reading by the side of the road – often I could manage a book a day – or my creative reporting of my exact position so that I could start an hour late and slowly 'catch up' throughout the day, getting stuck in imaginary traffic jams until by lunchtime I was where I said I was and where I was supposed to be. I was like an urban Donald Crowhurst. Crowhurst had falsely reported his position during a round the world yacht race in the late sixties. He kept an imaginary log which he hoped would convince race officials. But when it came time to rejoin the race and sprint for home he lost his nerve, or his sanity, and committed suicide. In my own small way, skiving and driving was doing me in too. I wasn't happy and yet I couldn't see a way out.

The Sun Also Rises

I was on the radio, bleating to Fat Jackie at base that the traffic on Bayswater wasn't moving. At the same time, without even indicating, I decided to bale out and make a U turn out of the mêlée of stopped cars into the free lane going the other way.

I turned the wheel hard, lurching across the centre of the road and in a blink saw a motorcyclist coming up fast on my blind side. With a slowed down dead certainty his bike hit the nearside wing with an awful crump of rending metal. Simultaneously I saw him flying and my windscreen stretching out of shape and bursting into a marvellous pattern of fractured vision. The motorcyclist flew, and I mean flew, before he crashed to earth in a crumple of dirt-stained hi-visibility vest and leathers. I thought then that I'd killed him but he got right up, swearing and shouting at my folly. At least he was unhurt. His bike and the van's front were a write-off, though I was just able to manoeuvre the thing back to the office. As I drove into the sun the light on the cracked screen cascaded everywhere into my eyes.

The Guinness Test

After the crash the boss issued an ultimatum that I should either consider my career prospects or ship out. I still didn't leave, but then five days later a terrible pain erupted in my left side. I walked out of a burger shop, took ten steps, and then the incredible surge of pain hit me, as if I was being stabbed by something very sharp. It was probably, I reasoned, a very severe case of burger poisoning. After a few days the pain went away. I even started jogging again.

After three or four weeks, though, I began to feel slightly groggy and there was a dull ache in my side. An unreasoning dislike of doctors and hospitals kept me from making an appointment at the local clinic. I wanted to tough it out like people did in the past.

In the end I crawled to the hospital, clinging to railings for support as I went, after a failed 'testing' session in a pub some hours before. The test was: if I could drink two pints of Guinness and smoke twenty Winstons then I hadn't got appendicitis. After the first pint and ten cigarettes I was beginning to feel very very queasy. In the hospital, after the operation, which happened the same day, they said that my appendix had already burst and had spread itself all around my insides and was poisoning me. I was lucky, they said.

Lying in bed I suddenly knew what to do. I would walk. I would walk myself better and I would walk out of my old life. I would do something I could be proud of for once. I would walk on my own the complete length of the Pyrenees mountains.

I told Shift It I was through with driving and at my leaving party Fat Jackie gave me an alarm clock as a leaving present.

I had always loved walking and walking was something I knew that I could do. A long walk would be a challenge, but a challenge at which I stood a better chance of succeeding than any other projected enterprise. The BIG WALK would be my challenge for the year.

The BIG WALK was from the Mediterranean to the Atlantic along the ridge of the Pyrenees mountains. The key to the whole thing, I knew from experience of shorter 'long' walks, would be boots.

Hemingway used to say that boots should hurt like hell for six weeks and then they'd be fine. Modern boots, such as Timberlands, promise to be comfortable immediately. Even boots are becoming softer, more feminised. I resolved to a get a pair of stiff old fashioned boots – heavy soled, big welted boots with leather laces. I didn't have enough time for extensive breaking in so I wore them around town as I worked out my notice, heavy footing the brake and the throttle and thinking of my escape.

After boots comes the rucksack, the defining piece of

equipment for the serious walker. Such a walker, with fully laden rucksack, presents a strange forward leaning aspect, his life on his back causing him to look at the ground or angle the head forward like a duck.

The rucksack is an alibi, a bona fide excuse for being off the beaten track. When I strayed on to private property wearing my big rucksack I always felt I had a right to be there. I was legitimately blown off course from my big and serious undertaking. I was no mere stroller. The rucksack becomes a companion, a friend. I understand why, even allowing for high altitude oxygen deprivation, Reinhold Messner wept when he had to dump his rucksack during a solo attempt on Everest. I too walked without human company but I never felt alone.

I could not afford the space for a tent so I took a nylon Force Ten flysheet, which, combined with my iceaxe and rucksack, made a very cosy little shelter. The iceaxe was never used for its intended purpose, since it was not very snowy that year in the mountains.

The other essential kit was moleskin (cloth adhesive plaster) for blisters and the tiny scissors that are part of a Swiss Army knife, which is an OK pen knife, though the can opener does have a tendency to bend under heavy use.

Boots

At first it was army boots that I loved, with their mirror finish on the toe cap and the sides of the heel. When an army sergeant-major taught me how to clean boots when I was a small boy I was inordinately happy. And though I never fully mastered the hot spoon and never quite got that plastic looking mirror shine, I always took care to polish the sole along the instep. My grandfather, who was a farmer, always wore handmade brown boots with toe caps and leather laces. Leather laces were definitely the business as far as I was concerned.

Boots are definitely getting less bootlike, less macho. They are lighter, smarter, apparently more waterproof, but they last months instead of years, and they do not stretch in the same way as leather because they are made from artificial materials.

If I'm going on a bit here it's because I want to really find out for myself why that walk seemed so important then, why it seemed so crucial that I not give up, when, after a hundred miles or so, my boots began to give me hell. HELL.

The Wall

Walking in crippling boots with a heavy pack in high mountains is not fun. Every step requires an act of will. Every stop is marred by knowing that one will have to start walking again, all too soon. Even the magnificent views seem poisoned, inked over with agony, seen through bleary spectacles of pain.

And passersby, fellow walkers one might have greeted, are ignored, hardly noticed by the trudging, limping hunchback, unmanned by every step he takes, his posture broken.

Napoleon was wrong: an army marches on its feet, not its stomach.

It was all my own fault. Having extolled the virtues of real boots, for a real walk, as worn, no doubt, by real men like Hemingway and me, I had failed to discover their true nature in the short time I had taken to break the boots in properly. Now they were exacting revenge with a cruel bastinado reminiscent of the finest inventions of a Persian Court torturer.

Breaking boots in is a mysterious process. One school believes that boots are *never* broken in. Instead it is one's feet, far softer and more malleable than leather and rubber, which are broken in to fit the unyielding boot.

The leather does stretch, creases do form in the upper, so something is going on. For some reason, though, if the boot is worn for an extended period of walking too soon (real boots, I'm talking here) something goes hideously wrong. The gentle period of acclimatisation is replaced by a chain reaction: the boot wears the foot in one place and when there is no reprieve it just gets worse and worse.

The problem was not blisters or pinching. This was far more serious: the back of the boot was biting into my Achilles tendon.

I tried wearing another pair of socks, cutting insoles made of karrimat material to raise my feet above the tendon-cutting heel. I tried even more layers of socks, then, in desperation, only one thin pair, leaving the boots loose. This was dangerous, given that I was carrying a high heavy load and the path was often narrow and above a great fall, but I did not care, I was past caring, limping into a half-hell where personal safety is just not a concern.

The Breakpoint

This was the point when I could have given up. With my sore feet, four hundred miles to go and only one hundred walked I could so easily have given in. In the end I arrived at a suspicious far distant village called Py, where the old people sat all day in the square watching with beady uninterested eyes everything a newcomer did. In the local *gîte d'étape*, a kind of hostel, I made a pair of flip flops from my yellow foam karrimat. The next day I hitch-hiked to Prades to buy some new boots, the kind that did not need to be broken in. It was really that simple.

You think, at the breakpoint, that superhuman amounts of energy are needed to keep going, but actually all you need is enough to get through and past the breakpoint. If you get past it your energy to continue is miraculously renewed and you think, 'How could I possibly have even considered giving up?' when only hours or a day earlier giving up seemed the most sensible thing to do and only pig-headed stubbornness kept you at it. But it is almost as if you have to accept the real possibility of failure before life lets you succeed.

Visions Of Bass

Somewhere west of Andorra I fell asleep on a flat rock during the hottest part of the day. When I awoke three deer were nuzzling the grass less than six feet away from me. With just one eye open I watched these normally so timid creatures act with complete unawareness of me. Then I moved, just slightly, and they all three stood stock still for a long second and then bolted, instantly out of sight, or so it seemed.

I lay on the warm rock thinking about Bass, a friend who had died only recently. Bass suffered from bipolar syndrome, the new name for manic depression, and in the end he killed himself. After he died all the incidents of his life seemed to thread together and make sense, though when he was alive those same incidents seemed without any special point or significance. He told me once that he had been out stalking in Scotland on the estate of a rich friend. They had stalked one particular stag all day through the rainiest, most unpleasant conditions. Finally, and much to the ghillie's delight, they found themselves on a low hill less than fifty yards from the grazing beast. Bass sighted up his rifle – he was an accomplished marksman and the whole thing looked in the bag. Suddenly and without warning he jerked the rifle up and fired way above the stag's head, which of course bolted. Then Bass started to laugh his huge mad laugh. The ghillie was furious and demanded to know what he thought he was doing. 'Doing?' snorted Bass, again breaking out into loud laughter, 'I wasn't doing anything. I was giving the world another chance.'

The Trials Continue

The new boots, though soft and accommodating, had cost a lot of money. Now my budget was slashed to the bone and I had to be careful about every Coke I bought and every bar of chocolate. It also meant I couldn't afford to dawdle.

Attempting to cross an icy mountain river that would reduce my walk by four kilometres, I took off my new boots and draped them around my neck. Half way across the torrent, which was raging around my thighs and threatened to pull me over if my stout walking stick slipped on the river bed, I decided, for no reason, or perhaps for the very slight reason of lightening my load, to fling my boots to the bank I was making for. The first boot landed safely. With an awful inevitability the second boot bounced on the bank and then slid off into the bubbling flow of the river, disappearing downstream in seconds.

Losing a boot in such circumstances is no time for tears, though I felt mighty close to it. I limped back to the near bank, dumped the burdensome rucksack and started to leg it barefoot down the bank. Running alongside the fast flowing stream I saw the pointlessness of my task. By now my boot would be half way to the sea. Increasingly there were brambles along the river bank and more and more of them were sticking into my soft, white, much blistered soles. I sensed the all too familiar hopelessness that precedes the delirious, though horribly temporary, euphoria of giving up, bunking off, running for home. I'd look round one more bend and that would be it. I limped on. Nothing. One more bend, the very last. More limping. Nothing. One more . . . was that a crisp packet lodged half submerged as the water dived like liquid glass around the dull egg of a rock standing midstream? The boot was caught. I inched towards it expecting at any moment for it to break free of its point of imprisonment by the divided current, but it held.

I dried the boot in the sun and laced it up and felt that happiness special to avoiding self-caused disaster. Not an inch further forward, back to square one, in fact, but strangely happier than before.

The Author Faces His Most Severe Test Yet

To reward myself for not giving up I splashed out on two nights at a superior *gîte d'étape* in Merens, about half way between the Atlantic coast and the Mediterranean. It was here I was accosted by the girl.

'You are taking the path west?'

'Yes.'

I'd already noticed the girl in the *gîte*'s communal kitchen. She wore a red bandanna around her head like an Indian squaw, though she had long brown ringleted hair and only lightly tanned features. She had a thick nose, bright eyes, a nice though determined outdoors kind of face. She wore shorts and had those wide hips some women have, where the triangle of light between their legs seems very obvious. Did I like that? I wasn't sure. Nice legs, though. Maybe my age or a little older. Mid-twenties. Her name was Marta and she was German, from Manheim on Rhine. She'd been in the Pyrenees before and knew the Dutch couple who were talking to me over a carafe of cheap red wine. Introductions were made.

Marta straddled the communal bench and looked me directly in the eye. 'I will be walking to the west as well,' she said.

'Good for you.'

'There are no accommodations on this route except for the empty huts of the shepherds.'

'For at least a week's worth of walking, yes.'

'So I will be walking with you,' she said, as if it was a foregone conclusion.

Er, hangabout, I wanted to say. I've only just met you and well . . .

'I'm quite a fast walker,' I said.

'So am I,' she twinkled back, smiling for the first time.

'I mean very fast,' I said.

'We shall see,' she said.

It was decided. I was walking with Marta.

She *was* a fast walker – going uphill – but downhill I always overtook her, and this was undeniably satisfying. Marta was an environmentalist, an ex-hippy acid-head and now an apprentice cabinet maker. She had a strange walking stick that looked as if a snake was curling around it; it was the result of a creeper enspiralling a branch, and this she told me was the symbol of an apprentice German cabinet maker. One month she'd been a hippy living in a squat and taking acid and the next month she'd got a part-time job, a flat and had enrolled as a trainee cabinet maker. 'You can change your life in a month,' she used to say. Then she'd give me her direct sincere look and I had to agree it was an exciting prospect, changing your life like that. 'But the hippies taught me one thing,' she continued.

'What?'

'They taught me how to love.'

I knew what the words meant and I knew sort of what she was getting at and, years later, I would know exactly what she meant, but right then I was slightly mystified.

We walked all day and at night stayed in the little stone huts that guard the highest hills of the Pyrenees. There was always water gurgling in a stream near these huts and every night Marta washed some item of her clothing and left it to dry over the fire in the stone fireplace inside every hut. By the third day I knew by sight all her knickers, her socks, her functional orange sports bra. It seemed like we were going about things the wrong way.

At night we talked about anything and everything as the wind whipped over the hills. Marta rolled her tiny Samson roll-ups and I smoked dry Spanish cigars and fed the fire with the odd pieces of wood we picked up during the day. We'd talked about religion, marriage, the mystical attraction of trees when finally, several days in, we got on to money.

'How much money do you have? For this walking?'

'Not a huge amount . . . I—'

'How much?'

'£300.'

'And this is to last you two months? It is not enough.'

'Well, I'm living very cheaply. I only stay in manned refuges once a week. I have my flysheet—'

'It is not enough.'

The boots had dented my wallet, it is true, but Marta didn't know just how penny pinching I could be. The idea was planted, though, and she gave herself over wholeheartedly to solving my perceived cash crisis.

The next evening she told me, 'I know a farmer near here who has fruit trees. You can pick fruit and earn money.'

'Good idea. But if I stop walking I feel I may be tempted to give up—'

'I will call him when we get to a village. I don't mind working too. I have his number with me.'

The next day we spent hours walking up and down boggy valleys, losing our way and then finding it. Marta didn't have a compass but she was much better at map reading than I was, I had to admit that. We only made nine kilometres despite walking for nearly ten hours. When we found a tiny deserted shack on the top of a wind-blasted hill we decided to stop.

The shack was full of a shepherd's supplies. There was no fireplace and the narrow sleeping platform was stacked with bags of salt. We moved the salt, laid out our sleeping bags and slept exhausted side by intimate side, the wind howling all around the hut, insanely flapping a piece of plastic we were too tired to do anything about.

A few hours later I awoke to absolute silence and calm. The wind had dropped to nothing. Through the tiny window I could see bright stars in the night sky above.

'Can you feel the magnetism?' came Marta's low voice out of the darkness. 'I am feeling the magnetism myself.'

I suppose it was bound to happen. But this wasn't like being at home. I had a purpose now and did not want to be distracted. I was grateful, too, that Marta was not too good looking or seductive.

'How do you mean?' I asked, though I knew what she meant. Shit, it would be so easy.

But I knew myself. If something started here, up in the remote hills, I'd be forced to choose between dumping Marta after one or two nights or leaving the high ground to go the easier way she planned on following. Maybe Marta was an emotional hard case and sleeping with someone was just another kind of exercise. I wasn't that tough.

'Are you feeling the natural magnetism?'

Miles from anywhere. Decent bird virtually throwing herself at you. Romantic hut on top of a mountain. Why not? I waited for her to make the move, take the decision away from me.

And yet I knew why not. The walk. The big walk. The challenge. My life. I felt like an early Christian mystic out on his spike of rock being tempted by all the earthly pleasures the sly old Devil could think up. I really saw succeeding at the walk as somehow indicative of succeeding at life. If I gave up . . .

Pedantry came to my rescue:

'Well, it's quite normal. Two people lying side by side. In close proximity. I should think the magnetism would be, er, normal.'

Marta sighed.

'Any people who spend time together and get on will develop a certain affinity that one might be justified in calling "magnetic" though perhaps a better term might simply be acclimatising to a new personality . . .'

Being German she didn't question my analytical turn. Being myself, a bit of a soft touch, I knew in my heart, the heart that was revealed very clearly up here in the bright starlit night, that if I moved even slightly towards her, lifted my hand from its place rigid at my side, I would be giving up. For a shag.

'I think I better go and check on that plastic,' I said. Marta said nothing.

Outside it was bitingly cold and clear. The stars spread out above me and there was no moon. The plastic had wrapped itself around a piece of barbed wire but there was no longer any wind to make it flap. I tramped around the darkened hut which seemed like a tent at the Antarctic. I was Oates going outside for 'some time'. A hundred yards or so from the hut I took a piss, the stream just catching the available light. Marta wanted to follow a longer and easier route through France. In order to save time I intended to go south into Spain following a harder more vertiginous path. If she wanted to come with me, fine. But I wouldn't go her way because I'd run out of cash and get sidetracked and then where would I be? Back on the vans?

When I got back to the hut Marta was snoring, an even-pitched snore, reminiscent of a small animal sleeping. I lay down on the hard platform next to her and went to sleep. Who was I kidding? I wasn't Casanova, capable of loving and leaving. It was the walk or the woman.

In the morning I showed Marta the map and my proposed route across the mountains. She matter of factly pointed out her route down through the valley. There was a momentary stand-off. I started to explain but stopped. Marta was smiling. 'I should give you a hit with my big stick!' she said.

We separated on good terms, and went our own ways.

The Sea At Last

And eventually I did make it. With six francs to spare, which I spent on a litre of beer.

Limping the final few miles down to the Atlantic coast at Bayonne I felt neither elation nor disappointment. 'So this is it,' I thought, sitting on the beach watching the big Atlantic rollers come pounding in.

I had been hatching various fantasies about what I would do, having conquered the full length of the mighty Pyrenees on foot. In the movie in my head I threw off my rucksack and stumbled into the sea praising the Gods for blessing me with success. But I could see it wasn't going to be like that – the beach was fairly crowded and if I carelessly chucked my rucksack down someone might steal it. Plus, my watch wasn't very waterproof so I'd have to hide that somewhere. All these preparations took time, and so, even when I was in the glorious cold sea, I only swam a few token strokes, since I was so keenly making sure no one stole all my gear.

I'd always assumed that success after a difficult struggle would be accompanied by a special success feeling, but it wasn't.

Death and the Rite Of Passage

The four challenges which characterise the primitive rite of passage are very much about confronting death. The killer inflicts death. The pain sufferer partakes of the most traumatic aspect of death, which is the pain associated with dying. The man who never flinches has learnt to 'stare death in the face'. And the man who has mastered a skill oftens finds that skill can be turned to killing, be it a martial art, marksmanship of a high degree, or the ability to make and use his own weapons.

Death and transformation are always linked, since the transformation of the self can be likened to the 'death' of the old self. In many mystical traditions one must 'die before one can die', in other words accept that the immature self must 'die' if one is to be transformed in this life. The primitive rite of passage emphasises the nearness of death and the requirement of death's nearness as a way of sharpening our appreciation of life.

The original notion of the rite of passage, which gained widespread interest in anthropological circles in the 1960s, quickly wore out its welcome in the academic world. It seemed highly appropriate, yet at the same time too vague and all encompassing to be a useful academic tool.

The external rite of passage, though, is highly recognisable. It may well be a part of our cultural inheritance that we designate some event in our lives as a rite of passage, as a way of making sense of our journey through time. As we have seen, this requires at least a modicum of belief in the counter-cultural perspective, but increasingly that counter-cultural perspective is becoming, if only informally, more and more widespread.

A writer might consider getting his first book published as a rite of passage; for someone accademically minded it could be gaining a PhD; for the mountaineer it could be making a first ascent of some peak; for a salesman it could be gaining those elusive keys to the executive washroom . . .

You see the problem: the rite of passage starts out as a useful tool and then gradually becomes so watered down that any kind of vague challenge seems to qualify.

It is more fruitful to return to the original primitive notion of the rite of passage as something concomitant with the death of the boy and the birth of the man through some real and observable external activity.

Such a 'personality death' requires that the ROP is either difficult or dangerous, with failure being a real possibility. If we admit of the possibility of a meaningful rite of passage for the modern man then it must be a difficult and dangerous challenge set in the world of action not reflection.

I'm backing myself into a corner with this extreme rite of passage reasoning. Perhaps the next step would be to suggest a compulsory National Service where young men are whipped and beaten into discipline by hardened ex-servicemen with a grudge against boys who have spent too much time in front of the Playstation.

But this would be just another 'top down' solution, more social engineering by the mainstream culture. The experience would be resented and negated by the context of state imposition. The modern state is so all enveloping already that a healthy response to a 'rites of passage initiative' would be to reject it. Besides, no meaningful rite of passage could ever emerge from the rule-bound committees that sit in the offices of power.

A modern rite of passage only works if you choose it, and not everyone will. The act of choosing makes it meaningful, and this is necessary since, however tough it is, if you think an ROP is meaningless then it will be. It will only work if it is part of the silent revolution, people who are quietly getting on and doing their own thing and not waiting for a top down solution. And that isn't everyone.

3.00 p.m.

After the cooking, a cake is brought out. Everyone eats cake and drifts in twos and threes to the corners of the garden examining plants and herbs we have planted.

I am congratulated for the shed I am building at the bottom of the garden which will be my place for writing, away from the foreseen disturbances of any noisy child. So far I've managed to raise eight thick poles in a circle with a skeletal apex of rafters joining at the top. It looks like a gazebo in the making, or one of those trellises for roses that you sit under on just such a warm summer afternoon as this.

I look at my watch. Sixteen hours until our appointment at the hospital. My wife seems very calm, chatting to relatives. I am all of a sudden nervous. A friend's mother is the unfortunate recipient of this nervousness when I rant on about how many diseases you can catch just visiting a hospital. She is a retired GP and expert at calming the likes of me. Though, ominously, she does say, 'Even if you have to have a Caesarean you can go on to have natural births later on. My first child was a Caesarean and the second and third were natural.' I feel queasy thinking about Caesarean sections but my wife looks composed, sipping at mineral water with a piece of lemon in it.

Small Game Hunter

It was a few weeks ago, when I was moving the wood for the shed to the bottom of the garden, that I noticed the pigeon was back. I had been watching this pigeon for a long time, maybe three months. For a while it lurked in the tall eucalyptus trees that overhung the garden, then it became bolder and took to flying down to the flowerbeds and pecking around. For the last two weeks it had taken to uprooting the tiny nascent herbs I planted in our nascent herb garden. This was the excuse I needed. The pigeon was eating our food. The pigeon had crossed some deep and elemental barrier: him or me; I had been given the green light to blow his brains out.

It is as if I need an excuse to do something I both want to do and am repelled by. Accurately you could say I think killing things for food is a necessary thing and by extension a good thing, a human thing. I want to think it is a good thing and have that reassuring 'good thing' feeling, the kind of feeling you get when you pick up the change dropped all over a shop floor by a doddery old person fumbling with their purse. I also know it is not entirely normal to want to kill things, but this is pushed to the back of my mind. I want to kill the pigeon and I don't want to kill the pigeon. I rush madly to get my gun.

Gun Crazy

The gun had been delivered by the postman in an anonymous brown box given away only by the gun logo at one end. I was alone in the house at the time, just me and the postman. I unwrapped the box in silence, not believing my luck. The gun was only an air rifle but it was the most powerful kind of air rifle you could legally own and had won numerous awards for its build quality, accuracy and so on. Often it was described as 'the industry standard for pest control'. That made me very happy. I was the proud owner of a professional piece of kit.

The rifle was very well made, with a blue steel barrel, heavy walnut stock, safety catch and hi-power telescopic sights. The whole thing was heavy and substantial feeling and looked like a real rifle and not a toy.

I pretended to shoot my neighbours, nosing the rifle barrel through the bedroom curtains, silent as a hit man staring down the cross-hairs of his 'scope.

Gun-loving Vegans

Many people dislike guns because guns kill people. But everyone I have shown my air rifle to, including a vegan who wears plastic shoes because leather involves killing cows, has exclaimed over the workmanship, the fact that it is a thing of beauty. I'm sure that its deadly purpose adds some dramatic edge to such workmanship, makes the workmanship look better than, say, the excellent workmanship on a super-expensive corkscrew. There is, at some deep level, a connection between the competence to make weapons that is exemplified in such workmanship and the weapon itself, as if weapon making skill is more skilled than other forms of manufacture. Look at the way people examine a top-quality cooking knife or a bayonet in a collection of militaria. They handle with care, and always exclaim about the workmanship. I think, in some deep long-lost primeval way, that there is a hard-wired link between making anything and weapon making, as if weapon making is the archetype of all manufacturing.

Rabbit Man

I tested out the gun hunting rabbits. As a boy I had always been unlucky catching and killing animals of any kind. I once lopped the tail off a squirrel I saw run over. Roadkill was about the extent of my hunting prowess in those days. Snares I set in fields, after instruction from my grandpa, who was a farmer, always caught nothing. Snares my grandpa set always caught everything. And every evening during the War he had gone out with his airgun and shot rabbits for the pot. When the War ended my grandma swore she'd never eat another rabbit ever again. And she didn't, which was a pity, because my grandpa loved them. But, as he always used to say, 'What the cook doesn't like the troops don't eat.'

I considered this rabbit-catching expertise my inheritance, something I would have to claim, sooner or later. When I got the gun, state of the art industry standard, etc., then there was no stopping me.

Friends who lived in the countryside invited me up with the sole proviso I did not shoot the tame rabbits in their garden, or the tame squirrel. In nearby fields I saw plenty of rabbits and resolved to go hunting the next morning.

I should say that by this stage I had wound myself up into a blood-crazed hunting frenzy, fuelled by reading numerous semi-literate mags aimed at airgunners like me. The gods of these mags were either field-target competition champions or industry professionals in the field of pest management. Pest management was given a lustrous, exciting aura, even though most of the time you knew the pest men were dealing with cockroaches and wasps. Rats, rabbits and pigeons were for them the real joy of the profession, what made it all worthwhile. It was then that they could use their guns. I read their tips with eager glee.

Game Reserved

After several early morning forays looking for coney (rabbits) I arrived at several conclusions: 1) rabbits run away very quickly, and when moving cannot be easily shot using a telescopic sight; 2) rabbits may occupy a field one day only to ignore it another day; 3) rabbits that have been 'ferreted' or hunted by industry professionals are cunning and nervous; 4) this was most of the rabbits in my neighbourhood, except; 5) the rabbits that lived in and next to a nature reserve.

Rabbits that live in nature reserves are tamer, bigger, slower and more trusting than rabbits that live in the real world. Slowly, irrevocably, I turned my attentions towards the 'reserve'.

Knowing that the public would be against me, I adopted rather sneaky tactics for operating in the environs of the nature reserve, which, by now, I had convinced myself was the only place I was likely to get lucky. I carried the gun in an extended backpack and when I was near the reserve I draped a camouflage net between two trees so that I would not be seen as I aimed down the sandy bank at the lolloping rabbits thereabouts.

Early morning or evening is the best time for coney, better still if there is no dew; rabbits are a lot like humans in that they prefer warm dry weather to getting cold and wet.

Behind my net I waited for the small game to appear. I should say, in my defence, that I was shooting into a field, which was traversed by rabbits that lived in the reserve but were greedy enough to want to eat grass in the dangerous outside world. By their greed I felt absolved from the hideous guilt of violating the natural paradise of the reserve.

Within minutes two rabbits were nibbling at the grass some twenty yards away. I sighted up, lying on the dirt, barrel extending through the netting. Slowly I squeeze. A considerable bang for such a quiet place; hope there are no early morning dog walkers out with their dog off the lead. However the rabbit I aimed at is still there. The pellet went over its head. The other rabbits scrammed but this one just froze for a moment and then bent down to start eating again.

In a fever of excitement I reload.

Bang. The rabbit flies backwards out of the scope's visual field. I look over the barrel and can see its dead grey bulk on the grass. I can even see very red blood on its head.

Now something almost like fear grips me. This is the first thing I have ever killed apart from wasps, fish, ants, mosquitoes and flies. I have never run anything over, yet, and even the fish I walloped as a kid were cold blooded, flippy and flappy on the bank, but not like a warm-blooded bunny, for Chrissakes.

At this point any industry professional, or even kid on a farm, is probably sneering. Well, I'll just keep going. This is how it was for me, urban softy man at the end of the twentieth century killing his first meat. And I've been eating meat for thirty years. I've eaten meat that has entailed the destruction of cows, chickens, deer, snakes, monkeys (monkeys!), not to mention pigs, sheep, goats and turkeys. But never once have I killed any of these creatures. I am, you might say, supremely out of touch with my larder.

But Bang, and it's done, and now I'm at one with my prehistoric past. And I feel a little fearful, just the feeling, it seems ridiculous. Even a live rabbit is hardly a dangerous creature. Even a rabbit that had been on the unfortunate end of radioactive contamination and had grown to five times its normal size would hardly be much of an adversary. But still that feeling, whose first cousin is fear, makes me walk carefully down as I go to examine the kill. I wonder if it isn't something primeval, a left-over from when men killed big dangerous animals armed only with spears, then moving in for the final kill or to check an animal was really dead, that would be the most dangerous moment.

I poke at the poor creature with the gun barrel. Of course it doesn't move, it just flops over, supremely relaxed, just dead. When I pick it up I'm surprised at how thin it is, not much meat here. Its dead weight threatens to slip through my hands. I force myself to tighten my grip, getting, at each moment, closer to the reality of this killing lark. Which now, in the cold light of dawn, is not much of a lark. I look up over the ridge of the nature reserve to the single-strand barbed wire and the grey open sky beyond.

Rabbit Pie

In front of my friends I am full of bravado and skin and gut the thing according to a book I read earlier. It tastes faintly unpleasant, as all rabbit does unless it has been marinaded a long while in brine. For some reason I don't go rabbit hunting in the nature reserve ever again.

Pigeon Pie

That was a year ago. Now I am looking down the barrels at the pigeon that has had the nerve to enter my domain, eat my herbs, violate my right to food. Because I am firing out of the top-floor window, opened with fiendish silence very slowly as the damn thing pecks up the mint, because of that I am actually very close to it, maybe twenty feet or less. Through the scope, set to 7X magnification, its sleek white-ringed neck looks easy to hit. I aim for the head, stop breathing and squeeze. A few fluffy feathers are kicked up as it falls dead to the ground in the herb garden. Again I get that stupid fear-like feeling and actually have a cup of tea before venturing outside to investigate. Still warm, my hated foe seems quite small once I feel through its puffy feathers. Vermin, I tell myself, but even killing vermin is not all it's cracked up to be.

5.30 p.m.

Everyone has now gone home. The washing-up is done, the barbecue embers doused (by my brother). I load the car in preparation for our early start tomorrow. We are supposed to be at the hospital at 8 a.m.

9.00 a.m. Sunday

We're already home! After hanging around in an upstairs reception area watching women in dressing gowns trail around drip supporters on wheels, waiting and watching we are told that the hospital is overbooked. We can check into the observation suite and simply wait, or we can go home and come back later in the afternoon. We gratefully go home.

4.00 p.m.

This time it's for real. I know that as we drive again the three miles to the marble cliffs of the hospital. As we drive up past the base of the building we pass a huge cavernous kind of open warehouse space, which is invisible from a distance, but seems to be a kind of maintenance chamber for pipes or a grimy garage of some kind. Whatever it is it occupies the entire ground floor of the hospital as you approach, and it seems to me for a moment to be the epitome of unwelcomeness.

I park the car and dither about how long a long-stay ticket I should get. I look at my wife, standing some way off, her longish skirt blowing in the light breeze, big now I can see. I buy the longest ticket – for Chrissakes, now is no time for cutting costs and being cheap.

Into the reception area. I've been here a few times before, just to drop my wife off and pick her up from the numerous tests she's been subjected to. We pass men in shorts and football shirts and women in shellsuits sitting around drinking coffee from the League of Friends cafeteria. I am overdressed and know it – pressed shirt, black trousers, shiny winklepickers I bought in New York – but at this stage I feel fine about this. Perhaps I also want the doctors to know I'm a good class of customer and not to be shortchanged just because I have a foreign wife. In the past I've had very good service from the NHS, even, you might say, preferential treatment because I was young and well spoken. I'm not so young any more, and maybe things have changed.

Bedlam

'Your hand's shaking, mate.'

I looked down at my hands as I absentmindedly stuffed tobacco into my pipe. They were shaking, not wildly, but noticeably. To me this was insignificant. Probably meant too much coffee and nicotine, nothing more. I was sitting in a shadowy fan-cooled restaurant in Bangkok, eating breakfast with Carol, a man I'd only just met.

'Couldn't help noticing, that's all.'

Carol said this with an intonation that suggested I was somehow less of a man because my hands were shaking, that somehow I had failed an important test, had been found wanting. He seemed a little sad for me, his new mate, whom he'd known for about an hour and a half. His new mate with shaking hands.

It struck me forcibly that the shaking hands thing hadn't measured anything since I was about twelve. At twelve shaking hands meant fear, incipient 'spazziness'. Carol was a forty-two-year-old coal-train driver from Queensland. It strikes me now that shaking hands probably is significant in the world of train driving. A shaking hand signifies a lack of nerve, or nerves shot to bits, or drugs and drink; certainly nothing to recommend a man who might have to hit the stop button at two hundred kilometres an hour.

My shaking hands condemned me as unmacho. It was a novel feeling. I hadn't been around that kind of machismo for years. It seemed almost schoolboyish.

After the Pyrenees I'd finally just taken off, travelling almost by whim, discovering that it was never as expensive as I had always previously thought. All the years I'd stayed in England and I could have been out in the wide world. It was only a half regret, yet it served to keep me on the move, determined to see as much as possible.

In the Cockpit Hotel, Singapore, sitting on the verandah at four in the afternoon as the rain came down like metal rods, I met Jeremy Bedlam, an English doctor working at an international hospital in Singapore. Bedlam took all his holidays in Thailand. Over several gin slings he told me about the women he had 'liberated' in Bangkok.

'If I didn't pay their bar fine, then they face being picked up by some horrible leering fat German sadist on holiday from Dusseldorf.'

Bedlam was my age, very blond, with a fit body and an unhealthy pallor. He was for ever dripping eyedrops into his eyes to make them sparkle. In his bathroom was a large bottle of mouthwash. I imagined an intractable ring of blackheads around his neck, just below collar height. There was always a pack of red Marlboros in his white coat chest pocket and he drank Asahi Superdry every lunchtime. Superdry, you can't smell on someone's breath.

Bedlam was recently divorced from his Japanese wife. Maybe he sought solace in Soi Cowboy (a street of brothel bars) and Pat Pong. He certainly made buying hookers sound like an act of kindness. That was one of his talents, bringing his unique, perverse, vaguely unbalanced worldview to bear on activities I'd thought were cut and dried, sewn up. Bedlam made out that prostitution in Thailand wasn't even really prostitution. You paid the girl's bar fine to stop her from being screwed by fat Fritz or that prat back from a Bahrain oil platform. That she went back to your hotel, well, that was only natural if you were as charming and good looking (though in a mean way) as Jeremy B. And if she should happen to sleep with you then that was OK too and giving her a 'present' the next day . . .

'How much?' I asked. I needed to know all the details.

'Up to you,' he said airily. 'Five hundred baht, maybe.'

Ten quid.

The present was just a custom. Cultural politeness to leave it. You had to hand it to Jeremy, he made screwing whores sound like a children's birthday party.

But when I got there I saw that he was right, in a way. The girls who parade up the bar top in King's Castle or Pink Panther look like students and the better looking ones like models. Some even have quite thick glasses, which is endearing. Their faces are not hard or wayward, like the faces of prostitutes in England. They look like normal girls.

And the bar fine seems reasonable. You're taking the girl away from the bar where she is an undeniable attraction. You should pay the bar manager for that. And the present, well, you want to pay, you want to be generous, you want to show your appreciation.

The whole thing seemed like an unfucked-up version of the one night stand, the singles bar without the need for lies. It was closer to that by far than twenty minutes in a sweaty cubicle off the Reeperbahn.

As you can see, persuading myself was not that difficult. But my first night in Bangkok I went to a restaurant recommended by the guide. I was only there for four days. If I hadn't met Carol then maybe nothing would have happened.

Here's how I met Carol. I walked into a post office where he was dropping some postcards off. He started talking to me with immediate ease: 'Been here five days, fucked six women, never wear a condom, pretty stupid, eh? Probably got Aids. What d'ya reckon?'

'Nah,' I said, since any other answer seemed judgemental at best. Inevitably we carried on talking after I'd finished in the post office. We agreed to have breakfast together. That's when he noticed my shaking hands.

Hemingway's Tool

Now that Carol had drawn my shaking hands to my attention, I kept checking them for shake. I discovered that if the wrist is resting on the edge of a table, the hand shakes despite this support. It is as if the nerves are reacting to being squashed slightly by being rested upon. The other check method I used was to hold my hand flat out in front of me as I looked across the back of the hand to detect any wobble. I found my mind at such times engaged in the useless act of denial. If I saw a slight wobble I'd wipe that check sequence from my mind as somehow unrepresentative and, with renewed concentration, both hold my hand still and check at the same time. There is something deeply illogical about trying to achieve some standard at something and yet at the same time judge yourself as having reached that standard. For example, when checking my pulse I always try to make it go slower at the same time by a kind of psychic osmosis.

It seems to me that this self-checking at the same time as performing is, essentially, infantile. Kids yearn, say, to be taller. So when they are measured they stand secretly on tippy-toe just to be able to say they are half an inch bigger than they really are.

Hemingway, too, is guilty of this hopeful check fallacy. He and F. Scott Fitzgerald were in the toilets of the Ritz Hotel in Paris. Fitzgerald has confided, in his cups, no doubt, that his thing is too small for his liking. He confides that he has a complex about it. Hemingway, at that stage still a consoler of men rather than a bully, tells Fitzgerald to flop his tool out so that Papa can take a closer look. Rather than being weird or kinky, I think this shows the humanity of Hem, his desire to get involved. I think it is endearing. Said dick is exposed. Hemingway pronounces immediately that it is of normal size. This, I suppose, means either of two things: 1) It is actually very small but so is Hemingway's dick so that makes it normal; or 2) It is normal size.

Whichever way you look at it, a crucial part of this anecdote is the size of Hemingway's tool. But to move to the punchline: Hem tells F. Scott that he's been looking at his dick from above, naturally, rather than front on or side on in a mirror. Side on, according to Hem (tested; it's true) the dick looks bigger than when you look down on it from on high.

Fitzgerald was only half convinced.

Now the interesting part. Only a man who believes his dick is too small would go to the length of trying to make it look bigger by studying it in a mirror. The twin facts that Hem was a) keen to console and b) knew a surefire method to make your dick bigger tells us that Hem himself was concerned that his dick was too small. Now, and we are entering speculative areas now (but what the hell), if we can take at face value F. Scott's concern, then that taken together with Hemingway's behaviour suggests that Hem's own dick was either not much bigger than Fitzgerald's, or that he considered dick size important enough to lie about it to console a friend, which again points to a concern bred from experience of a small dick himself. Either way you look at this anecdote, America's two greatest twentieth-century writers both come off, sorry, with small appendages. Add this to the whole dick amputation concern in Hemingway's work and you get an even more damning portrait of the man's equipment.

Returning To the Point

The point I have deviated away from, albeit, I think, fruitfully, is that Hem suffered from the same infantile urge that made me check my shaking hands in order to stop them from shaking. Dicks are either big or not, examining them in a funny light doesn't add a millimetre, unless . . . unless it is the perceived length that is important, rather than the real length. In other words, one wants to *look* a man, more than wants to *be* a man. Isn't this Hemingway's grotesque and fatal flaw? And I mean fatal. Didn't his love of appearing a 'real man' eventually do him in? Take the drinking. He drank because of a 'nervous disorder'. Hem's image of himself was of the kind of man who wasn't nervous. So he drank to eradicate a part of his mind that did not fit with his preferred image of himself. But the drinking damaged his health. By that stage he couldn't give up: Hemingway had become the mask. Maintaining his ego was more important than maintaining his body. Hem was now Papa, Hemingstein, the great writer; in other words, externals. The dick-size thing was symptomatic, if I'm not overloading the anecdote too much with this observation: it showed a man more concerned with how he appeared than how he was.

Like a movie actor. Like a politician. Like a beautiful woman. Like someone who lives in the age of mirrors, movies, television, advertisements.

Bangkok Nights

Carol suggested we went out on the town with his friend, Karl, whom he had just met in the lift of his hotel. Karl had a portly figure and a goatee, reminiscent of a German doctor of philosophy. Karl ran a business sending antiquities back to Gottingen from Bangkok. He recommended the girls of Soi Cowboy over other places. 'They are checked for the disease each week,' he explained.

In the fumy, humid evening, before going out on the town with Karl and Carol I checked my shaking hands to make them stop shaking. And sure enough, in bad light, held outstretched, my hands no longer shook. I was a man again, whatever Carol thought.

At this point I should say that Carol had mouth ulcers caused by the extensive braces on his teeth. It was new to me that braces were even possible for a man of Carol's age, but apparently they were. Carol also had a tan, dark hair, was tallish and drove an open-top Mustang or some such car. 'At my age,' he admitted, 'you need at least a Mustang to pull girls on the Gold Coast.'

This should have alerted me to the flaws in Carol's character. In fact, it did, but he was also a friendly bloke and fun to be with, so I didn't think about it.

The only thing that really disconcerted me about Carol was his stomach. He was tanned, as I said, and with a shirt on his stomach looked flat. But without his shirt (he took it off in his room as we shared a beer) his stomach looked grotesque. It was both flat and flabby at the same time, puckered rolls of tanned flesh sort of smeared around his waist. It was a fascinating sight. I wondered if a Mustang cancelled it out, whether it mattered?

Carol chose his whores badly. They were always trying to wriggle out of the deal, allowing him 'one fuck only' or acting bored and pissed off when he wanted keen and swooning. To my unpractised eye the girls he picked were obviously no good, right from the word go. Carol seriously lacked judgement. He also chose girls who spoke no English, which wasn't necessary, as plenty knew quite a lot of English. Worst of all he chose girls who were obviously greedy for money.

My own girl told me she had started as a bar girl only the previous week; an implausibility I was happy to believe. There was something sad about her, a reluctance to even ask me for a whiskey, and she could speak English. She told me she had given up working in a department store to become a bar girl. With luck she earned in three days what a store girl earned in a month. She smiled her sad smile and accepted an orange juice. Within three days I had half fallen in love with her, was planning ways to help her. I wasn't any good at this prostitution game, I wasn't wired right for it. I was too damn discerning, I told myself, too damn soft.

I left for the airport at three in the morning and she was still sleeping, so I didn't wake her. I left all my spare notes on the mantelshelf. 'Whatever you want to give,' she'd said, which made it easier.

It was dark in the road outside the hotel. I stood there with my small rucksack, waiting in the cold for a tuk tuk scooter cab. After a while, one pootled by. He gave his throttle a good revving when I told him I wanted to go to the airport. Then I was speeding on my way in the back of the draughty machine, the cold morning air sluicing over me, and the ever-present smell of exhaust mingled with it. Speeding out of town in the pre-dawn time, glad to be on the move, escaping that feeling of sadness, if only you can move fast enough, leave early enough. Important not to think too much about any sadness you may have caused.

Talking the Walk

From Bangkok I flew to Japan, where it was possible to earn money very easily teaching and rewriting English. I began living in cramped circumstances with an overweight Iranian called Fat Frank. I was twenty-eight years old.

Fat Frank was the first person to bring to my attention that I 'did not have a walk', meaning. I did not have a habitual and recognisable way of walking. He told me that everyone in his village back in Iran had perfected some kind of trademark walk by the time they were eighteen. I was baffled. It never even occurred to me to counter that the only people who had 'walks' in the England I'd grown up in were what my father called yobbos: feet splayed, gut or testicles thrust forward, chin inclined as if resting on chest, the only movement side to side, exaggerated, a walking sneer; slow paced and inefficient as movement, but effective, very effective in articulating a self-regarding insolence, a lazy fuck off to all and sundry.

Perhaps crap culture was more prevalent in Iran, or more likely, macho culture. Frank's own walk definitely had that insolence about it and a not to be hurried quality.

My father was keen on walks with a military bearing. He and my grandfather both walked as if they were marching. Sometimes I slouched, sometimes I walked like Giacometti, sloping into an imagined wind, sometimes I remembered my back injury and walked very upright. What Frank objected to was the variation. He saw something unformed in me, studentish, despite my twenty-eight years, a man who presents different postures to the world depending on how he's feeling. How you feel, thought Frank, was secondary to the task of a man, which is to impose himself on the world, encircle a piece of turf, be it only that on which he happens to be walking, and call it his own.

Tim's Walk

My attempts to change my walk started with observation. I noticed Tim, another teacher, with his shoulders hunched up to make him, I imagined him thinking, broader and more impressive. The actual effect was to so raise his centre of gravity that he looked like a top-heavy bowling pin waiting to be toppled. We usually have such a poor internal idea of our bodies that when we try to change something we end up making it worse. This had happened to Tim, his raised shoulders conveyed apprehension not power.

Active Principle

What follows may be bollocks, so be warned.

Fat Frank used to describe people using verbs as nouns – he's a passive, he's a timid, she's a brave, like that. He said that, in general, adolescents are passives; men are actives. This had no sexual connotations, and even had nothing to do with the quantity of activity – a passive could have lots of energy and move around a lot, be very active, in fact. Rather it had to do with one's attitude to experience. A passive cares mainly about the quality of the experience, its novelty, thrill effect, ability to move. An active cares more about the effect they had, how effective they were. An active wants to be succeeding, but also in the absence of success requires, in the manner of nutrition, the feeling of being successful. Fat Frank was always the hero in his stories. He always saved the day, he always *did* things. Things didn't just happen to him, and those that did he wasn't much interested in.

A passive accepts he probably can't have any effect. He accepts his powerlessness, and sits back to enjoy the ride. Whilst a passive doesn't enjoy being mugged, it doesn't disturb him too much: 'It was a real experience,' they'll be able to say later. Most grown-up men, by contrast, find mugging a humiliating experience, it somehow means they're 'not men', it offends the active principle in them.

One function of a rite of passage may be to turn passives into actives.

Empire Of Spine

What interested me was that by simply doing a different walk I could completely change my state of mind, transform myself into a different person almost. It was as if I was learning again what I had forgotten after my climbing accident. We think we have one area of life nailed, but then we haven't and life comes round and shows us we haven't. What I had forgotten was that a new walk activates a different self. And this new self has adventures inconceivable to the old self left behind.

Stung by Fat Frank's gibe I went from learning to walk to studying aikido, which reinforced notions about posture's importance.

A Japanese girl said to me that all English men have a gap between their collar and their neck at the back because they are always slightly stooping.

It could be that the differing postures of each nation gives rise to the way that nation thinks about itself. It could be that the decline in England's cultural confidence can be read in the collapsing spines of the middle classes. Certainly the Japanese stand and sit differently to us.

Another Thing

It is a truth of mystical writing to assert that every thought has its counterpart in a bodily movement. If you want to change your mind, change your body, or the way it moves. Posture reflects a state of mind; it also creates a state of mind. Slumped forward the mind begins to wander, feel drowsy. Forcing oneself upright, back straight, the mind begins to function again. Similarly, a walk can restore one's calm, one's perspective on a problem, even aid solutions to a problem. The body walking has its own mental counterparts, its own sympathetic dendrites, neurotransmitters and receptor sites, all creating a different mental landscape for each move we make.

Christophe's Walk

Christophe, a Frenchman studying Zen and aikido, used to wear wooden *geta*, sandals, in the depths of a snowy Tokyo winter. The cold never bothered him. He was always cheerful and walked with his chest puffed right out in front of him, enjoying everything life might have to offer. Christophe's walk was like one continual deep breath taken and held to demonstrate healthful living on a lovely day. Until I met Christophe I had no idea of the extremes a walk can go to. My vocabulary of walks was monotonous and limited. Not that Christophe's walk was silly, it wasn't. Before I met him I thought I stuck my chest out when I walked upright. No way. I was *slouching* compared to him. I was frightened I might impose if I walked so obviously having a good time. And it's true, one annoying aspect of the United Kingdom is that many people are openly affronted if you seem to be enjoying life too much. Maybe it stretches back to the classroom, where the 'hard' walk ruled and the timids had to slip by unnoticed. Christophe taught me not to care. Walk as if you think it's the most beautiful day in your life, as if you haven't a care in the world, as if you harbour only good will to all. And pretty soon it will seem that way.

A Few Things I Learnt In Japan

In aikido the whole point is to learn to control your centre of gravity. Top masters can shift their centre to where they want it: at their end of their finger tips or down in their feet, and this, I can assure you, is no exaggeration. If you hold a baby and keep holding it as it falls asleep it will feel noticeably heavier. This is because, when relaxed, its centre drops to a lower point. If you hold a sack from underneath it feels lighter than one gripped just by the top: the weight is the same but the centre of gravity in relation to our effort is different. Centre of gravity depends on rigidity of the skeleton, which depends on tension in the muscles. The more tension, the higher the centre. Aikido concentrates on developing awareness of body tension so that control can be got over the centre. For a long time I thought aikido was about being relaxed. This meant giving myself a hard time for being so stiff, so unrelaxed. But when a Westerner, an Anglo-Saxon, is told to relax he just goes soft and wobbly like a hippy after a severe bout of inhaling. This is as ineffective as being tense.

The sixties were all about chilling, relaxing, not getting uptight. What better definition of a high centre could there be than 'uptight'? But in an effort to lose this 'uptightness' people adopted 'relaxed' poses – formless, floppy, ignoring posture, defeated. In fact, once you chill out, you are already beat. Instead of 'relaxing' into useless postures of indolence and defeat all that is needed is to shift the centre away from the head. To do that certain muscles must be less tense than others, but first must come an awareness that the centre exists, and that the centre can be moved.

5.30 p.m.

We've seen the midwife, my wife is wearing a nightdress and lying in a bed and the sun is shining in through the window. We've seen no doctor and I assure my wife this is normal. 'We don't over medicalise birth here like they do in Egypt.' It's true, that in Egypt you get a lot of reassurance from the doctor at all moments of a medical procedure – but then you are paying for it.

My wife is hooked up to a machine that measures the heartrate of the baby inside her. The machine often 'loses' the baby for minutes on end. At first I panic, but the midwife assures us that this is normal, the baby moves and the machine loses track of it. I decide I don't like the machine.

A Reason

I started aikido because it didn't seem as violent as kickboxing or kung fu. It was known as one of the softer martial arts. Women did it. But though I professed a dislike of violence, I didn't really know what I was talking about. I thought violence was what happened on Saturday night when some pissed idiot gets his nostrils joined with a swipe from a spent glass. Or when a rugby forward thinks he's off camera and decides to plant a stud into someone's kidney, or when eight New York cops open fire on a frightened man in a doorway and turn his body into a string bag of flesh.

I didn't see violence in the way a hammer gets nailed into wood by an expert carpenter building a house. Or the way a tree is felled or meat butchered. But all these things need violence, controlled violence. Violence is at the heart of aikido, just as it is with any martial art. That violence is a combination of muscular power and a narrow, focused, amoral, devoid-of-sympathy mental stance. If you want to knock someone's teeth out don't start feeling sympathetic as you wind up the punch.

People who are deficient in feelings of pity and sympathy are often better at violence than those who are not. This helps give violence a bad name. In fact it's a tool for getting things done, sometimes an inappropriate tool – you can't climb a rockface using violence, punching your way from hold to hold, it just doesn't work that way. Violence is an explosion of unfettered power with no thought of the consequences, it's giving it your best shot. But it's still only a tool of limited application, not that useful most of the time.

Mostly when people go on about violence they mean inappropriate violence, situations where the violent are exercising no self-control because of drink and drugs. Lack of control is what we should deplore, the inappropriateness of the violence, not the act itself. Fortunately many people who would be violent in this inappropriate way lack the physical capacity and courage it requires.

To deny violence is to deny something powerful inside all human beings, more so in men than in women. And by denying it in ourselves we cease to understand the world.

Mind Over Matter

The Japanese ninth dan Takeno Sensei used to say the strongest position for a fighter is to say, 'Welcome, give me your best shot,' not 'Can I have him or not?' or even, 'What if he kicks high or tries to headbutt me?' The 'welcome' posture is not a head posture. The centre is lower, away from the judging, criticising part of the body. Which is good, because we don't fight with our heads, we fight with our bodies.

And all fighters agree, you can only be any good at fighting when you cease to care that much about winning or losing. Most people who 'hate fighting' are surprised that a punch isn't that bad; a kick, though painful, is forgotten in a few days. They don't really hate fighting, they hate the idea of losing a fight. They're frightened of losing, of being humiliated. More 'head' postures.

Kamae

Kamae is stance, posture. Fighting stance; posture ready to do combat. *Kamae* is the body's version of the fighting mind. Every misfiring neurone is represented as a deficiency in *kamae*. Just as the head-based centre will show as a top-heavy *kamae*, so more subtle failings in thinking will show up in bodily posture. A man who looks as if he can't be thrown; that man knows something valuable too.

R'spect

Unless you have felt real respect for someone you are likely to dismiss the whole concept as hypocritical and bogus.

Further, someone you really respect may also frighten you, just a little, just enough to make it confusing.

Lack of respect is also a fruitful topic. Young people, especially nowadays, generally lack 'respect', i.e., deference. Each new generation lacks even more respect than the one before. Adults, finding kids too rude to deal with, keep their hard-won knowledge to themselves. So each generation has to reinvent the wheel in many areas. The one benefit of this situation is that hypocrisy is reduced; having to 'respect' useless old gits becomes a thing of the past.

If one demands respect one might usefully ask 'What for?' For being old? For having survived?

Men want r'spect. They really do. Black culture has reintroduced the concept into the fashionable end of the mainstream. But the r'spect offered is like our 1950s politeness, only hipper.

In the present ethical vacuum there is only real respect and nothing. Real respect doesn't need to be broadcast, cannot be demanded, is pretty much a private thing. It would exist even if there were no name for it. You see it in martial arts or during a crisis, places where people reveal themselves. Indeed, it can only exist in difficult testing situations, or rather the qualities that are to be respected can only be revealed in difficult testing situations.

Tattoo You

A tattoo is painful and lasts for life, a Red Ferrari is expensive, working out is a drag. There may also be a simpler, less permanent way to get this all important macho attention. Why not wear a fake tattoo from time to time? Hire that Ferrari. Put shoulder pads inside your jacket.

There is a whole range of pretty useless male activity which could be called surrogate masculinity. It's doing things you don't want to do to get this all elusive respect, attention for being a man.

To recap: men like a certain kind of attention. This attention is rarer today than before. Men have to go to greater extremes to get it. But these extremes are those of display rather than real action. This is because opportunities for real testing have largely been removed in our safety conscious world.

Fear is the Key

I am not a frightening person, which is probably a good thing, but once, when I had large healing cut on my face, I found that people in the street didn't want to look at me for too long. Even burly street beggars looked away, as if I might have given them a good kicking. Obviously the healing cut on my face (which came when I was hit by a falling piece of wood I was trying to nail in place for the shed I was building) made people think I was a fighter. They were frightened and looked away. So now I knew the origin of looking hard and cutting your hair skinhead-short and getting tattoos and all the rest. It's to make people slightly frightened of you.

Heijoshin

The Japanese use a word, *heijoshin*, which loosely means inner moral worth or the-conscience-that-is-acted-on. Inner moral worth is a hard thing to pin down – a lot of it has to do with courage combined with sympathetic sensibilities, to be compassionate and yet also courageous. It is easy to demonstrate varieties of courage during training. A good teacher can highlight these for the student. He can also demonstrate compassion, but then it is up to the student whether he learns from this or not. Martial arts may not force you into being a better person, but it can show you sides of yourself you did not know and probably do not like and may therefore want to change. Sports do not provide the same opportunities because all is forgiven in sport if you win; how you behave is very secondary. In Japan, how you behave is important, so the atmosphere for improving oneself already exists in the dojo.

Art Of Standing

During a photoshoot for an article about aikido (this is after I returned from Japan to the UK) the art director told me, and a few other aikido practitioners, what he wanted to photograph. I could not help watching the way he moved. He was not an old man, maybe forty-five, maybe less, but he moved with a curious hesitant stoop, as if he had been so long acting this weird jerky walk that it had finally stuck with him. It was a movement designed for moving from a seat to leaning on a desk to sitting in a car. I could see in his unsteady need for support from the walls and the furniture a kind of devolution forced on man. He had become homo sedentaris – though not fat and slow, his movements were quick, birdlike, but also hesitant, off balance, like someone acting old, or convalescing from a broken leg, except he was perfectly well. This all contrasted with his hip, glib, sarcastic speech. His voice was the cynical voice of the journalist who thinks they've seen it all, peppered with words that are favoured by the young: 'cool', 'sorted', 'can't be arsed', 'safe'. I could tell that he thought of himself as 'young', certainly not of the older generation. In a few years his body really would be old. He would have managed this transition straight from young to old with no time in between.

Facing Death

How you face death is the constant theme of all *budo*, war arts. The fact of dying is secondary. We will all die, so do not worry about it. Think instead of how you will face it, whether you can really die as you live, a smile on your face, making a joke with the man about to behead you.

In many ways all this extrapolation about being a man is a circling of the idea of how you face death. It is a dance around the fact of death, which echoes the great Victorian explorer Sir Richard Burton: 'Life is a dance along the icy brink, but should that make the dance less fun?'

The Issue

I've been skirting the issue, hiding from some unpalatable truths, skimming over my time in Japan, claiming to myself I've written it all before in my book *Angry White Pyjamas*. But I haven't. The fact is that I had a hard time doing the year-long aikido course with the riot police in Tokyo. In fact, I had the hardest time because I was technically, in many areas, the worst performer. What made it even tougher, unnecessarily tougher, was that I spent most of my time trying to learn with my head.

Excepting periods of exhaustion, I was so keen not to make mistakes I did not trust myself to just 'do aikido'. As a consequence I made basic and obvious errors, because you learn aikido with your body, not your head.

Nervous about making a cultural gaffe, worried about

making a technical mistake, fearful of injury: my overwhelming desire to finish actually handicapped my ability to do so. For a year I learnt aikido almost despite myself, snatching in techniques when my body and brain had given up caring, driven way past exhaustion point. But a year of this and you pay a price.

Once I stopped the incredible amount of exercise I had been doing I was no longer ever physically tired. Tiredness had been my only way of relaxing. Now I had none. For a year after I finished the course I had to perform a complicated series of relaxation exercises, sometimes twice, before even attempting to go to sleep.

I had thought, in the moments when such a thought didn't seem ridiculous, that 'the course' would make a man of me. Instead, although I was confident physically, I was mentally way out of shape. In a pub, if someone knocked into me and didn't apologise, I'd get nasty until they apologised or someone intervened. When a beggar importuned a friend by reaching for his lapel I grabbed the beggar's throat and screamed in his bemused face, 'You're fucking dead.' But these kind of incidents did not make me more confident. Sometimes I'd take taxis rather than walk through areas of town I'd never had a problem with before. It was as if, by doing all this training, I now had a responsibility to fight anyone who crossed my path; at the same time knowing that this was stupid, and therefore forcing me to take exaggerated action to avoid such situations.

Distant Mountain Viewing

A few days ago I was cycling quickly along the busy road in town back from the gym where I now practise aikido once a week instead of three times a day, weaving with style and finesse in and out of cars in a line waiting to turn, but remembering all along, for the first time in ages, to practise my Distant Mountain Viewing.

Distant Mountain Viewing is a martial arts exercise and means looking with the eyes focused on the furthest distance, with the eyebeams, as it were, pulling one along. It is intentional looking forward rather than passive recording. The whole field of view is registered with Distant Mountain Viewing, not just things as they come into one's immediate physical vicinity.

It's something similar to the idea of 'length of vision' in cricket. As a kid, playing cricket I used to wait until the last minute before reacting with a kind of flinch to hit the ball. My reactions were fast, and sometimes I magically hit the ball well, but mostly I was caught out by not watching the ball with an aggressive mind, a forward moving mind. Mostly I got bowled out.

Zipping along, seeing everything as falling into perspective some way behind the furthest I can see, my mind questing forwards, not judging distances consciously but kind of sensing them with my body, I know now that in some way I am prepared and won't flinch when something unexpected comes at me. Why can't I remember to do this all the time?

Nude Shaver

I should say some more about the gym because in many ways it features quite large in my life, since I'm often thinking about 'not going to the gym', probably more often than actually going, or even thinking about going. It somehow looms in my life. It's a brand new development for the area, more a sports centre than a gym, a hangar-like building which contains a luxury swimming pool, a hi-tech work-out room with clinking chrome weight machines, multiple TVs and a computerised work-out system, a fancy bar finished out in light Swedish style birch-wood, and the most luxurious changing rooms I have used. Usually changing rooms are a let down, however good the gym or dojo is. In Japan, the changing rooms were completely functional – four large alcoves of grey dusty lockers, three showers and a row of sinks. Above the sinks a mirror. No benches, no carpet, no frills.

Even the other fancy gym in town has a pretty ordinary changing room – metal lockers but with more mirrors and benches to rest your tired butt on.

This gym is different. The lockers are all made of wood ('exquisitely crafted' some brochure would have it, but they are actually all the same), turned out by machine, but still wood, and nice to look at. Each locker is operated by a £1 coin. I've never used more than a 20p locker before. Somehow the pound sets the high-class tone even more, not that a pound is a lot in absolute terms, it's just that in locker terms it's a lot. Everyone I take as a guest comments on the expense of investing in a locker – even though, of course, you always get your money back.

There is both carpet and and an expanse of lino, for hygiene reasons, no doubt. There are mirrors everywhere. Everywhere – I'll get back to this. In most of the locker alcoves, except the one where I always get changed, there are square TV screens relaying CNN news and other irrelevancies. As well as the TV noise a vague piped music permeates the whole gym, probably loading us with subliminal adverts, though I can't be sure.

Actually, this vaguely sci-fi, detached, inhuman, corporate feel is what I most object to in the place. It costs money to use the gym and you have to be a member, and everyone who uses it is middle class and desperate not to appear as if they are so untogether as to have to actually talk to anyone else, except to say excuse me politely when you get in their way on the way to the showers. But even politeness is at a minimum in this place, people preferring to squeeze out of the way rather than open their mouths. The staff are all friendly useless schoolleavers on low salaries. They wear uniforms and do the minimum with a pleasant smile.

I may affect to despise the middleclassness of the gym users but I also really admire their dedication to fitness, the punishment they mete out to themselves, the sweat they pour, the miles and miles of useless running machine belt they pound, the hopeless kilometres they pedal on stationary bikes. I admire all that Victorian willingness to suffer. The gym is probably the last place in the West where sacrifice, discipline and pain are really understood. But after persecuting themselves with another useless bout of exercise the gym users just slope off, usually alone, avoiding all eye contact. I can't understand that.

Despite my obvious, indeed, growing dislike of the place I go there every week with my friend Chris to practise aikido. I went about a year hardly doing any aikido and I felt bad about letting this skill, which had cost me so much, lapse through inactivity. The hi-tech gym has several dance and workout studios. One has judo mats, which we use when the place is vacant.

After we have used the mats, done our aikido and convinced ourselves that we are improving, we go back to the changing rooms. The 'stiffs', as I call them, take a certain well-concealed amount of interest in Chris and me, dressed in our white pyjamas and black belts.

Back in the changing room we get changed surrounded by young middle-aged men who often have their kids with them, whom they take swimming. These men are nice guys with the pale unused bodies of successful office workers. There are also a few youngish turks, blokes in their early thirties who play five-a-side football or squash and still have reasonably muscled bodies. Chris and I probably look like them. And that would be OK had there not been, over the last few weeks, a new and unwelcome intrusion. I call him the Naked Shaver. Chris doesn't mind him as much as I do, but even Chris, who is exceptionally mild mannered, is driven to remark about the tactics of Nude Shaver (his name for the guy, which has, over time, prevailed) every time we leave the gym.

I can feel myself beginning to over-react. I can feel a real rant coming on. All Nude Shaver does, in effect, is to shave in the nude in front of the huge mirrors. That's not a crime. He doesn't insult anyone, or hurt anyone, except, except . . .

Nude Shaver is medium tall, has an excellent bronzed, slightly Latin-looking body, biggish dick, obscure tattoo on shoulder, black hair, model's Latin features. I heard him speaking once and he sounded South American, or maybe Italian. In any case I have never ever seen anyone literally strut so much. I knew he could not be English because even the hardest hardnut would have the piss taken out of him for strutting like that. Only in the supernice and supermiddle-class expensive gym where everyone pretends no one else exists could such a cancer as Nude Shaver's personality spread. For a start he whistles. Not a whistle of good cheer, or unselfconscious busyness, but an intrusive whistle of harsh tunelessness that is simply there to announce, 'I can whistle but you lot are too timid to whistle.' His whistle lets you know that Nude Shaver is in town. God knows you can even hear his whistle in the showers.

Nude Shaver has a leatherette bag of unguents, foams and potions that is as large as a small suitcase. This rests on the surface where the basins are, in front of the massive mirrors. He lathers up, totally nude, his dick just level with the bottom of the mirror. As he shaves you can see in the mirror his one eye or the other, depending on which side of his face he is shaving, beadily fixed on the whole gym changing rooms. His eye is looking for contact. His whole taut bronzed body begging for people, men, to look at it. He may be gay or he may be straight, he may be bi – actually, I don't care. Whatever his orientation, it is massively overwhelmed in significance by his incredible self-love, his omnipresent narcissism.

Chris stares at him, but it has no shaming effect. The guy loves it, struts away from the mirror to do a little tour of his domain, the locker rooms, the water fountain, the drinks machine, foam still lodged like war paint on his high, fine cheekbones. Every breath in the place, it seems, is held, waiting, restraining to exhale, 'What a tosser.' But we keep silent. He imagines, probably, that we are the beaten ones, slightly flabby, embarrassed middle of the road men whose only nude excursion is to the showers, who cover up, most of the rest of the time, not out of fear, but out of a consideration for others. Not Nude Shaver. His position, at the middle mirror, out there in the front, flashing his dick, his well-developed pecs, his flat stomach – all that with one aim in mind: to get into everyone's faces as much as possible.

After much thought I have come to the reluctant conclusion that there is no solution to the problem of nude shavers in the modern world.

6.00 p.m.

My wife has been given the first of the drugs that start the process of the induction. As we wait patiently for the contractions to start I suggest she listens to Bach cello suites on the portable CD player I bought specially so as to create a relaxing birthing atmosphere for her. She dutifully puts on the earphones and listens. Looking out of the window at the rest of the hospital, the ambulances arriving at A&E, the beige uniformity of the room we are in, the bleary plastic water jug, much used and much washed in the industrial hospital dishwashers. This is never going to work, I tell myself.

Staging one's own ROP

Staging one's own ROP sounds silly and artificial, similar perhaps to those hippy theatre groups in the seventies that staged 'initiation' rituals involving burial alive and 'resurrection' out in the Montauk woods. The thing to remember is that we do it anyway. By this I mean we structure our lives around such central concepts as an ROP. In the absence of one that is difficult and dangerous and therefore truly fulfilling of an ROP's requirements, people will shoehorn any part of their lives into the designated slot. It could be an illness, an adventurous holiday, a period of immoderate sexual activity where it is skill at hunting that is emphasised rather than affection. But instead of the experience being an accident that one later dignifies by the name of a 'learning experience', my own belief is that one should construct something that satisfies one or more of the ROP criteria and then set out to achieve it.

I could give a long list of potential 'rites' – from rounding Cape Horn to mounting a two-year bug-hunting expedition to the Matto Grosso – but the list would only reflect my own interests and obsessions. More to the point it would detract from what I think is as important as the testing nature of the 'rite' itself. This is the actual decision to subject yourself to some kind of test. Self-reliance must come quite high up the list of qualities that define being a man, and choosing your own test is the first test of self-reliance.

If you buy into this line of thinking then it's up to you to find a challenge that is difficult and dangerous. As a benchmark of seriousness, though, one should pay at least a little attention to the qualities needed to kill a lion, survive being hunted down by your own tribe whilst naked and covered in white paint, or remain smiling and unmoving as the witch doctor bifurcates your penis with a piece of chipped flint . . .

6.30 p.m.

My first cigarette break outside the front of the hospital. The air is warm and summery, a lovely evening. More men enter the hospital wearing clothes of extreme casualness. 'Huh,' I think. 'I'm not like them.' Why this should matter, I don't know. It's beginning to nag at me that I'm not the best person for this job. My wife wanted me here, so I'm here, though I can see that I'd much rather be down the pub, as my father was, when I was being born. I wouldn't want her to be on her own, of course. What I'd like would there to be a posse of highly experienced friends and relatives of my wife's all here in support. In medicalising birth the knowledge that women have gained over the centuries has been sidelined. The process began centuries ago in our culture, though only a few decades ago in Egypt. Men, who know nothing experiential of birth, become the experts, displacing women, who largely seem unfazed by this takeover of their traditional role.

I stub out my fag and pop back to the room. My wife's contractions have started and there is a new midwife to be introduced to. While I was away there has been a change of shift. The new midwife is Canadian and talks in a dull monotone. As she goes about her business fitting my wife up to a drip she speaks into a tiny tape recorder, like a coroner dissecting a body. When she discovers my wife is from Egypt she does the Indian *namaste*, hands together and bowing forward. My wife and I exchange raised-eyebrow looks, since this kind of bow is unknown in Egypt. Our smugness soon disappears when the Canadian midwife, who is short, stick thin, with a utility haircut and thick glasses, starts to ask obviously irrelevant questions relating to my wife's medical history. My wife answers as best she can and the midwife then intones a precise version into her tape machine, which makes my wife's answers sound somehow stupid. My poor wife, all hooked up to machines, looks helpless. 'Not good,' I say to myself. 'Not good.'

Under Fire

Back from Japan, I was living at home with my parents, which at thirty is a bitter pill to swallow. I was now more ruthless with such feelings, justifying my return to the nest as a logical way to save money while I attempted to fund my way out to the remote places where remote peoples lived their authentic lives, or so I hoped. Journalism seemed an easy way to travel and make money, though no money making occupation is easy at first.

It took a lot of dreary, continuous effort, plus buying the necessary electronic equipment to appear 'professional', but after that I started to pick up magazine commissions for stories related to the martial arts. Hemingway always makes his journalism seem so effortless, even when he is young and unknown. I mean the effort in getting a commission to write an article in the first place. It was never like that for me. For a long time it was tough to get work.

It was during this dispiriting phase that I went on a stag weekend with Chalky, Dave, John, and other friends I'd known for years. Dave was getting married and we chartered a deep-sea fishing boat to take us out into the Channel. The night before, we went drinking and consequently felt terrible the next day as we stood on the jetty looking down dubiously at the oily little tug boat we'd hired. Fortunately, it was too windy to reach the three miles offshore to be technically 'deep sea' so we simply trolled for mackerel and bream in the estuary, no one getting to sit in the Hemingwayesque 'fight' chair bolted to the ship's deck. I was the only one who didn't catch a fish and this seemed to emphasise the unsuccessful phase I was going through. Everyone mercilessly took the piss out of me and, for once, it really stung. Just as we were motoring back in Chalky hooked something very big and strapped himself into the chair. After nearly half an hour of reeling in he finally landed a thirty-pound tope, a kind of shark with razor-sharp teeth. Just as we were hauling the fish up the side using a giant landing net I felt my insides turn over with a gigantic lollop. In a second I was puking over the side, unfortunately right on top of Chalky's startled fish. Sharks don't blink, but as this one got covered in a heavy spray of partially digested chicken korma, I think it would have wanted to. Even after we'd dunked it a few times in the sea the vomit still adhered and no one really wanted to touch it. In the end, though, we did persuade Chalky to have his picture taken holding his spew-covered shark. After this low point, things could only get better.

I managed to get my 'overseas assignment' to India to write about its many indigenous fighting arts. It was there, in Bombay, that I met the female war correspondent. She was short, slight, short sighted and had been in every major war zone in the last ten years. She had made clandestine forays into Afghanistan in the eighties. She'd been in the hotel in Baghdad while the town was being strafed by the allies, she'd done Bosnia, Croatia, Macedonia and Sarajevo several times over. She was the last 'man' out of Mogadishu, and the first one into Rwanda during the Tutsi massacres. She even had a black belt in Tai Kwon Do. No doubt she could break boards and headbutt ice blocks into smithereens, but I wasn't asking.

This seemingly fragile dark haired woman had many times been 'under fire'. Casually, she described the arbitrariness of the thoughts one has as one is being shelled, how one can be thinking about having to get some more shampoo even as the enemy are lobbing their mortar bombs and trying to kill you.

I'd never been under fire. Suddenly and for the first time it seemed important. Yet at the same time I knew it was all bullshit. I knew that the 'me' that survived a good shelling would just be the same as the 'me' before, bar the odd chance of shellshock and deafness. You've had your ROP I should have said to myself. Any more is simply being greedy. And, besides, what about that primitive tribe you were so set on finding?

But at the back of my mind was the nagging question: would I flee from the guns or stick my head gaily above the parapet like those brave officers in World War 1? I didn't know.

The Four Ways To Enhanced Male-being

Whether or not one subscribes to the possibility of a modern rite of passage, there is still some mileage in adapting the challenges of a primitive rite into guidelines that enhance male-being activities. The four ways are:

1) Choose danger over safety.
2) Choose exteriority over interiority.
3) Choose pain over comfort.
4) Choose self-reliance over helplessness.

Every one one of these ways is, by the standards of the mainstream, aberrant, if not downright irresponsible. The mainstream is almost defined by its rigid demand that the only 'normal' response is to choose safety, comfort, interiority and helplessness (of course using euphemisms such as 'doing the responsible thing' for helplessness and watching TV and shopping for interiority).

In order to feel alive one must risk something. Simply turning up the volume only works temporarily – eventually over-stimulation causes stress, not the desired relaxation. People avoid risk and danger through the pursuit of stimulation, but it is a dead end. Without risk we cannot employ our most human attributes, without risk we are simply rather poorly designed machines for carrying out the orders of others. Our human superskills, unrivalled by any computer, include intuition, perfect timing, immense creativity and flexibility, the ability to heal others, the ability to inspire others, the ability to predict the future . . . all of these are possible only when we are in difficult, testing and dangerous situations. It is well known that huge physical exertions have been made by those alone and faced by someone trapped under a car or heavy load of some kind, physical exertions deemed 'impossible' by usual laboratory experiment. The whole point is that a laboratory is not where life happens, and life is flexible and dynamic, not mechanical and static – it responds to necessity not desire. In a tight situation we learn to trust ourselves, our bodies and our minds. Deprived of those difficult and dangerous situations we learn to distrust ourselves, lose confidence, lose our superskills.

We must risk our lives to gain life. This is not foolhardy when you realise that the human organism is a survival expert. It is not a piece of computing machinery that will stop the moment it gets a cup of coffee spilt on it. The human organism has been surviving for aeons and our superhuman skills are called forth in demanding survival-type situations rather than the dull drudgery of everyday life.

War Stories

As in most English families, both sides had been in the various wars of this century. On my father's side this stretched back to his great-grandfather, who'd been a redcoated guardsman, and on his mother's side even further back.

My father and mother, like most normal parents in the 1970s, did not encourage me to join the army. The army was all right in wartime but no place to be in peacetime. My father cunningly drew a picture of the extreme tedium of peacetime soldiering without actually counselling me against joining some branch of the armed services. By sixteen my boyhood obsession with the army had completely disappeared.

At university the only people I knew who joined the forces were either misfits, gay, honouring some ancient family tradition or teetering on the brink of a nervous breakdown. The tail-end of hippydom and a vague leftwing agenda was the conformist path.

Anyway, I didn't join the army. There was also the fact of Northern Ireland – I didn't want to go and get killed in a place where I wasn't wanted.

At the same time, *Dispatches*, by Michael Herr, was required reading. This confirmed that war was a kind of superior spectator sport, in which watching was elevated to a kind of participation through the reporting of that war. The heroes of 'Nam weren't soldiers, they were Tim Page and Sean Flynn riding into battle on Honda trail bikes armed with Nikon cameras and Tri-X film.

Hem Again

Hemingway confessed that as a young man he wanted 'to see war', just as Tolstoy's quixotic joining of the Russian army had been prompted by a theoretical interest in courage.

But Hemingway knew that you had to get close to the front

to get a good view. And being brave, he was prepared to take whatever punishment came as he pursued the spectacle. But still he was in that tradition of spectators of war, which goes back to antiquity; as late as 1870 the wealthy could pay for the privilege of watching the battles of the Franco-Prussian war from convenient nearby hilltops.

Something complicated drew Hemingway into his appreciation of war and bullfights. He wanted to watch, to observe and admire men displaying courage. He stated that he wanted to watch because that was 'his material'. But he also admired those men who were soldiers, yet he did not become one himself, so his admiration was not a simple thing.

In the modern world, war is far from being a simple duel between well-armed adversaries. In fact, to generate the commitment needed to fight a modern war, something like a state of madness has to be induced in both sides. Perhaps it is to Hemingway's credit that he could never submit to that kind of madness.

But still he hankered after situations in which to display his courage, both under fire and in front of the horns of a bull.

Courage is the Password

Hemingway's alluringly brief: 'Grace under pressure' is absurdly narrow as a definition. Aristotle defined it better: to say what courage wasn't was more useful than to point to courage itself.

The problem with any definition of courage is to know the inner state of the man 'under pressure'. Since courage has two components – the behaviour and the inner state. In public life the inner state tends to be ignored. Behavioural notions of courage are cultivated by society to best serve its own needs, rewarding foolhardiness and bravado, for example. We carry those notions within us, and perhaps question them as we question other societal imperatives that may have no particular benefit for the individual.

It is hard to dissect some act to find out if it was courageous rather than foolhardy. Our definitions of foolhardy are culture bound: amongst the Nagas, a tribal people, who, along with the Afghans, resisted domination by the British, there is no concept of an honourable death in battle. Men killed heroically are not even given a warrior's funeral. There is far more kudos attached to a raid which ends with a successful running away to fight another day. Courage, amongst the Nagas, amounts to daring matched by knowing exactly when to pull out.

The Japanese have an opposing view – for them the self-inflicted 'useless' death is the epitome of courage. Rather than be captured the traditional *bushi* (warrior) response was to commit suicide.

In the West we are somewhere between these two extremes. For us, courage does carry overtones of competence. With competence comes knowledge of how to be effective. But too much contemplation renders one unfit for action, where the split-second response is required.

There is a time element to courage. Some men, once they have 'psyched themselves up', are extremely cool and courageous. Those same men, if surprised, might surrender immediately. Are they courageous or not?

My Peculiar Obsession With Being Shot At

One of the first articles I wrote came from a tip from a war-reporting friend. He suggested I take a battlefield first-aid course and write about it.

Part of the course had involved crawling towards 'injured' colleagues whilst 'snipers' fired rifle blanks at us, as we ducked out of cover. It was just like playing army as a kid, except the blanks fired at us sounded like real bullets. I crawled so close to the ground my chin ploughed a 'V' in the leaf litter. Really I should have stopped there, this was as 'under fire' as anyone needs to get.

Posse

I spent time with a sheriff's posse in Arizona, trailing around in police cars, apprehending prostitutes and other suspicious characters. Everyone was armed to the teeth. I was given firearms training, shooting off everything from a .44 Magnum to a navy issue Thompson submachine gun.

Holding a pump-action shotgun to my shoulder and shooting at a metal plate target twenty-five yards away and hitting it I could tell the instructor still wasn't happy. 'Lean into the shot more. Take that target. Give me some aggression. Hit that target, hard.'

For these guys, retired policemen teaching civilians a thing or two, the gun is not just an instrument, to be used with neutral precision, it is part of, an extension of, the fired up fighting soul.

Voodoo

Later, in Haiti, where every night there was a background of sporadic shots, I spent most of my time on the hotel verandah drinking rum and feeling rather brave. A human rights lawyer told me no trip to Haiti was complete without seeing a dead body. Guns were everywhere. Even in the toilets at the main police station there was a bath full of M1 carbines, confiscated from one faction. But the only shooting I witnessed was a cat being killed by the hotel guard. I was coming back late at night and saw the muzzle flash before hearing the almighty bang. I hid for ages behind a tree in the darkened grounds before jumping out of my skin when I felt the guard's gentle hand on my shoulder. Then I saw the huge grin on his face and the dead piece of skinny grey fur held by the tail. I later heard he'd thought the cat had been a *loup garou*, an animal possessed by an evil human spirit.

9.00 p.m.

The little Canadian midwife has just inflicted huge pain on my wife by using a vicious little pointed stick to ineptly break her waters. Tipped with blood as it goes swiftly into the swingbin waste disposal unit, I think, this can't be right. The hormones are starting to kick in now in a noticeable way.

The problem is, for me, that I am reduced to being a handholder, a comforter, nothing more. This, I know, is hugely necessary, but I am unfit for the job. Most men, I guess, are. I want to get to the bottom of the situation, solve it in some way. But there is no solving, just waiting. The shoes are pinching. I should have worn a shellsuit.

Hard Access

In Haiti I met Andy. Andy was a new breed of war correspondent, a 'hard access' cameraman. He worked alone, used a modified DVD camera and relied on contacts with the world guerrilla network to get him into situations no official crew could ever hope, or usually want to penetrate. He'd been to all the usual places but always on the wrong side, behind the lines, operating with groups known for their antipathy to the West. Many human rights groups have informal connections with the fringes of terrorist and guerrilla activity. Andy used these connections and had a track record of making news clips that showed things from the guerrilla angle, be it in Sri Lanka, Colombia, Bosnia or, as in his bizarrest film, operating undercover with Tyrolean separatists in Austria.

Andy sold his news clips through a video news agency. When I met him he'd just come back from three months in Burma with various anti-government groups. He made his expenses plus about fifteen hundred pounds for each month he'd been there; very little compared to the fees garnered by normal TV reporters. But money didn't interest Andy.

In Burma he'd heard about a group operating against the Indians but based inside the Burmese border. This group was composed largely of Naga tribesmen from the north-east region of India, an area under military occupation since Indian independence. No one had ever filmed this group operating against the Indians. Andy wanted to be the first.

I had been interested in the area for years. It was where my father had grown up; before Indian independence my grandfather had served in the Indian army as an engineer in that region.

The Naga peoples in the hills between India and the Chindwin river were among some of the most remote tribesmen in the world. Cut off by politics they used flintlock rifles and still, reputedly, took heads. The guerrillas based amongst them were more advanced in the weapons they carried, supplied in the main by China.

Contacts

From a first contact in the bar of the School of Oriental and African Studies I met members of a human rights group indirectly involved with the movement to liberate north-east India and West Burma from the yoke of central government oppression. They vetted me and, because I was a journalist and had a family connection to Nagaland, decided that I was OK. I'd read a lot about the situation and knew what I was talking about, and the possibility of publicity for the cause was welcomed. With a security dependent on never speaking on the phone or writing names down, I was provided with contacts in the world of guerrilla activity. I flew out to Bangkok to meet the leaders of a guerrilla group that could spirit me into the land beyond the Naga Hills.

We met in squalid hotel rooms with multi-segmented mirrors on the ceiling; big, foetid rooms with fans and metal gauze on the windows to stop the mosquitoes, the kind of place I'd stayed in years before on my jaunt into the seedy world of bar girls with Carol, the coal train driver. This time it was very different. Bangkok seemed even noisier and more choked up. Everyone was fearful of Aids and no one talked about getting laid, certainly not the guerrilla leaders who were all staunch Christians. Staunch Christians who kill people, I had to remind myself. Only one of the group acted tough, wearing dark glasses and an easy, insincere smile. He was the political boss. The military leaders were polite and gentle, giving no outward impression of the numbers each of them had killed. One bespectacled ex-general spoke about his first ambush. 'I'd heard the British expression, don't shoot until you see the whites of their eyes. I told this to my men, those who were to start the ambush. The patrol of Indians came closer and closer and no shot was fired. Of course it was nearly dark and my men were taking things too literally. Finally, when I was about to be trodden on, they realised they'd never see the whites of their eyes so they opened fire.' Then he paused. 'I was very nervous. That was my first time to shoot someone.' With his round glasses and grey hair slightly sticking up he looked like a college lecturer.

Everything went very smoothly. A plan was hatched involving codewords and hook-ups in Rangoon and a complex but, I was assured, failproof method of crossing Burmese army lines into Nagaland.

On the last day it all began to unravel. The political boss was behind it. All the specifics, the highly specifics, we'd agreed before were now only confirmed in the vaguest of terms. It was still fine, they said, but of course it was not fine. All the times and the places were now 'we will have to see' or 'we cannot be certain'. A day before it had all been very certain.

On the plane home I kept thinking one thing and then another. If they didn't trust me how could I trust them? And the political man, I'd have to cross his turf on my way in and my way out and I could tell he did not like me. I had heard stories of the cars and wealth he had amassed on the legal side of the border; he was doing very well out of the situation, a journalist might upset all that. Maybe. That was the thing, I just didn't know.

Then I met Andy. He wanted to go. I had the method to get in. We could work together. Nothing simpler. By this stage I'd formed a loose agreement with a UK based documentary company. Andy said they were crap. We could form our own company, keep the money we made for ourselves. Andy was very pushy and very persuasive. Originally from New Zealand, he had worked until he was twenty-five as an accountant in the City. Then he threw it all up, bought a camera and headed off to Bosnia. The only clue he gave for being prepared for such a complete change was having raced stockcars when he was young. 'Loved danger, yeah.'

Now he was thirty and ready for more danger. He had blond hair, dyed black after his last Burma trip, and he'd have to dye it again if we managed to get in. I felt a bit of a heavyweight around him — he was tall but lithe, full of a nervous zapping energy, persuasive but very singleminded. He had a vague sympathy for any anti-government group and this was a salve for his conscience.

We met in noisy chain pubs in south London, all the secrecy being pretty good fun. Andy was really pushing me to make the trip. He wanted to believe we could do it. But he hadn't seen the political boss's eyes.

'Sometimes you've just got to trust these guys, fuck it, we're on their side, after all.'

Andy obviously had bigger balls than me. A wide open smile. Blond roots just showing. In the end I agreed. We would go in together. He would shoot the film, I would do the interviews. Then we'd split up and he would leave with the gear and I would leave with the film. 'They're less likely to be looking for you, at the airport, I mean,' he explained. Carrying a videotape of insurgents through Rangoon airport. Hmm. But I agreed to do it.

149

The best time to go was the dry season, which wasn't for several months. I began to prepare myself mentally (i.e., worry). I bought myself some jungle boots with special vents so that any water was pumped out with each step. I bought ripstop cotton jungle trousers, US army issue, and a civilian khaki shirt. Unlike normal war reporters hard-access journalists always wear combat gear since one side always wants to kill them. I thought about the female war reporter. 'I'd show *her*,' I thought.

Large Bollux

Andy said we'd have to finance the trip ourselves, that way we'd make more money when it came to selling the footage. I thought that I could combine making the film with doing some articles about the trip for magazines and newspapers. I spoke to the editor of one of the new 'ladmags' that had taken articles from me in the past. This softly spoken, bespectacled high priest of lager, tits, widescreen telly and football was vaguely interested in an adventurous piece about the Nagas, but didn't like the look of the expenses. He was much keener on something closer to home: bullfighting. He handed me a clipping about England's only matador, Franc Evans, and suggested I got him to train me. 'Training – that's more your sort of thing,' he said. Perhaps as a consolation he added, 'If "bulls" works out maybe we'll send you to Nagaland next.'

10.30 p.m.

My wife is now in considerable agony. She wanted to go through with the birth without having to have an epidural anaesthetic but now, between blasts of pain, she tells me it's much, much worse than she imagined. 'Shall I get the CD player?' I suggest, but I know as soon as I suggest this that it is a hopelessly silly suggestion. Normal contractions work their way through the body for up to a week before the birth. These chemically induced monsters have gone from a standing start to near full-on in less than five hours. No wonder the pain is immense. And no one told us. No one told us. Of course we had all the usual stuff but that was for a normal birth, not a power assisted one. The midwives just look at us and ask us what we want to do and we look at them and ask them what we should do. I know that despite the caring, sharing talk there is a plan afoot, a method for maximising baby production in this monstrous factory of life and death, and it seems a further injury that we have to suffer this phoney atmosphere of 'choice'. My wife asks for the epidural.

Hemingway Complex II

I'd been to bullfights in the past, and thought *Death in the Afternoon* Hemingway's best book. The first time I saw a bull killed I didn't like it, but by the sixth I was beginning to admire the matador for his bravery and skill and the killing didn't have the same impact. I saw a matador gored and suffer the indignity of having his trousers half pulled off at the same time, blood welling up in the crack of his behind. After that I knew the fixed look of courage on their faces wasn't fake.

I had run with bulls released into a stadium in southern France, but only one of the crowd, a studious-looking man with round glasses and a rolled-up newspaper, managed to claim the two-hundred-franc prize for touching the bull's horns. He did it and hit the bull on the nose with the paper for good measure. I was well out of the way, spending most of the time behind the heavy oak *barrera*.

I had never been to Pamplona, though a friend of mine had. He got drunk every day and only ran the bulls once. 'It's like the Christmas sale at Harrods,' he said. 'You don't know what's going on.' More memorably he had met an elderly man whose main claim to fame was that he knew Hemingway and had indeed been punched by Hemingway during a brief brawl during the mid-fifties. 'Actually, I could have killed him,' said the man. 'But out of respect I just let him knock me down.' My friend asked the man to punch him, fairly softly, just so that he could say he'd been punched by the man who had been punched by Ernest Hemingway. The man refused but after my friend bought him several Soberano brandies he suddenly whacked my friend right on the nose. 'Yep, that's about as hard as old Papa hit me,' he said. I asked my friend to give me a light whack just so that I could say that I had been punched by the man who was punched by the man who was punched by Ernest Hemingway. Strangely, he too was reluctant, as if he sensed that by punching too freely he would be squandering this magical Hemingway blessing that had been bestowed on him. But, weeks later, after a lot of goading, he did punch me in the stomach, quite hard actually.

The Last Battle

Franc Evans, England's only qualified bullfighter, agreed to train me in the art of being a matador. After this, I kept telling myself, you need never prove yourself again, that's it.

He took me to a school playground near his house so we could have more space to practise. He stood and whirled the pink cape, showing me how to make *suerte*, passes. He showed me how to rest the heavy pink cape on the practice wooden sword we were using. I was wearing my impact-resistant 'sports glasses', with curled sides to prevent them falling off my head in a moment of flurrying action, or if I got tossed by the bull. It was my plan to wear these same glasses during my 'fight' in Spain.

Hemingway, of course, had been short sighted, though most of the time he took care not to be photographed wearing specs. It didn't suit the image he wanted to project.

I didn't like wearing glasses either, but I'd been saddled with them since university days. Though there have been many bespectacled men of action, ranging from First World War air aces to the near blind adventurer Aubrey Herbert, there have been notably more men of action with perfect eyesight.

It comes down to the look again, the eyes; the warrior has it in the eyes. Somehow that is spoilt if the eyes are peering through two small panes of glass.

There is the inconvenience factor too. The glasses might drop off just when you need them. Or the fact that in a fist fight they are likely to be the first casualty. And there is the implied weakness of glasses. Although, perhaps to make up for all of this, I have known many spectacle-wearers who notice more, look more carefully than men with perfect eyesight. I am not, unfortunately, among them.

In a way I've always felt I've been sheltering behind my glasses. I see it sometimes in the faces of others, the fact that the glasses have become windows on to a world they are not part of. It's true that when you remove glasses, especially small-framed ones, the world suddenly seems wraparound near; you feel in that world rather than viewing it. But this feeling does not last very long. Eventually you are back to how you felt before.

For sensitive souls the cry of 'four eyes' is too much. They buy contact lenses and suffer all the red eyes and accidents with sinks and toilet bowls associated with that particular advance in optometry.

I thought perhaps that Franc might comment on me being a bespectacled would-be matador, but he didn't. In the playground I practised *suerte* using the cape and sword. These were heavy and after a few passes I had to rest my arm. Matadors must have a lot of strength in their arms and fingers.

When we started up again the right lens in my glasses suddenly popped out on to the ground. I immediately started grovelling around to find it. When I explained what had happened, Franc growled, 'You don't want that happening in the bull ring, do you?'

I would have to face this beast without my glasses. Franc had decided that after my 'training' I would face a horned cow on the ranch which often supplied animals to the bull rings where he fought. If I fought a bull then it would have to be killed, that was the law, because a pre-fought bull supposedly knows too much to be safe. Cows are not restricted in the same way. You can fight a cow any number of times. And these old cows can be dangerous. Franc had been gored in the anus by a cow. The horn had punctured his bladder. 'Would've died if the ambulance hadn't had a fast driver,' he said, in his low-key, almost quizzical way.

Franc produced a shopping trolley with a bale of straw in it. He pushed the trolley and I stabbed into it with a sword, a real one this time. It felt terribly theatrical. 'It isn't when you're out there,' said Franc.

The killing is the thing, the hard part of the fight. It's when the matador is most at risk, leaning over the bull and sliding the sword into the bull's neck. Getting the right spot is important – if you hit bone the sword can spring right out of your hand.

I knew also that the killing would be hard just because it was the killing. A few sick people like killing things, but most don't. They have to steel themselves up.

Needless to say, though I'll say it, these thoughts were far from my mind as I grovelled in the dust of the playground floor to find my glasses. Franc had dyed hair. He made no secret of it, even telling a story about how he fought a bull in Salamanca in the pouring rain and the dye from his hair ran down his face like ruined make-up. He wore waterproof dye after that. 'Fuckin' hate grey hair,' he said, and I could tell that he really meant it. He was forty-seven but with a thin active body, not at all the body of a former rugby league player, which is what he had been, but really the body of a matador.

In a way he was a fantastic eccentric. He made a living as an entrepreneur, with businesses ranging from a nursing home to a kitchen-fitting company. His father had been a butcher. 'That's why I didn't mind the killing so much,' he said, and I knew what he meant. My great-grandfather had been a butcher and whenever I was chopping up big pieces of raw meat just thinking about him overcame the potentially distasteful act of butchery.

Grey Hair

Franc's hatred of grey hair reminded me of my own, increasingly grey head. I started to go grey when other men start to lose their hair, and it had seemed pretty funny at the time. In fact, I was proud of the distinction my grey hairs accorded me. But there is a mysterious point, when the grey-threshold is crossed and you really look grey, old, definitely not-young. I noticed that a good sun tan can offset grey hair and put off this grey threshold-crossing point almost indefinitely. But I knew what Franc meant: that combination of pallid skin and lank greying hair – you really look old.

I didn't articulate my elaborate theory of masculinity at that point, partly because I hadn't yet thought it up, and partly because Franc was an action man, no nonsense, preferring action to mere words. I kept my counsel and just observed.

The Bullfight

Until the rules of bullfighting were formalised in the latter part of the nineteenth century the ritual killing of the bull was a dangerous business, a very definite test of a man's *cojones*. Bulls that were not killed lived to fight another day, and what a bull learns in fifteen minutes facing his first man in anger can be enough to make him a real killing machine. There are accounts of bulls eventually being turned loose on the range after dispatching ten or eleven men over the years. Such an animal has grown so wily that it can only be killed by shooting it dead with a powerful rifle.

Hemingway's discovery of the bullfight and its subsequent spread in popularity coincided with a turning away from such spectacles amongst most Spanish intellectuals of that time. The bullfight for them was an ugly, brutal reminder of a peasant past. They were anxious to modernise. Hemingway, coming from the most modern country on the planet, had already been modernised and didn't much like it. For him the bullfight was a challenge to courage comparable to being at war.

He ran, on several occasions, the bulls at San Fermín in Pamplona. This is potentially very dangerous. He never faced a bull armed with cape and sword, though he speaks in *Death in the Afternoon* of being in a ring with young cows and grabbing their horns as they charge, and being lifted and carried along by them.

He claimed he always needed a good drink to get up the courage for such antics. He also knew that drinking slowed you down and this was another reason he gave for never taking up real bullfighting.

Bad Vibes

Ever since 'taking this assignment' (i.e., begging the editor to let me do it) I was afflicted with a strange presentiment of death, or at least serious injury. At first it was damn unsettling and almost unpleasant. I took to asking people, 'Do you think I should do this thing?' Since most had no idea what it entailed they mostly said yes, since, in my experience, it's not that most people don't care about you, it's just that they don't have enough information to care about you, they just don't know where you are coming from. And in this case that was right. I mean, if you approach a guy whose job is sitting in an office and making phone calls and watching a screen to see how far certain indices have moved, and who plays tennis for relaxation, what is he going to say if you ask him, in all desperation, 'Should I fight this cow or what?' For a start he won't know that a cow is potentially more lethal than a bull and you are fighting the cow because it is cheap and possible. Second, he won't know what Franc's son told you, which is that being tossed by a cow isn't much fun. Franc's beefy rugby playing son was tossed by a small cow in southern Spain, just like the one I was going up against.

10.45 p.m.

The anaesthetist comes in and he is a bit of a lad, very chatty. He rolls out his kit, which is in pre-packed sterilised form, and slides on his thin latex gloves but does not wash his hands first. I remember the article I read about infection being spread by surgeons too arrogant to wash up any more. He isn't a surgeon, but where were his hands last? Scratching his arse or widdling the last drops of piss off his todger? And that way of putting on gloves without touching them – it never really works, I know from putting on rubber gloves covered in paint, some always adheres somewhere. Does it matter? Can the spine get infected by a dirty-handed anaesthetist? I don't know. Maybe I should have read up about it, but after reading *What Your Doctor Won't Tell You* I was so paralysed with anxiety-inertia that I just left it all to my wife, trusting the system; they'd never done me any harm. So far. Things have changed. There are more pointless tests now, and more machines, and more law suits and antibiotic-resistant flesh-eating bacteria, and doctors, I keep reminding myself, are recruited because they got good A level results when they were eighteen. Almost all those I knew who studied medicine whilst I was at university were easily brainwashable academic cannon fodder. I have only once met a doctor who has struck me as a healer – and shouldn't that be a better criterion than being able to do multiple-choice chemistry questions? I look at the dirty hands and say nothing. The monster needle dribbles and then goes in and my wife, quite soon, is out of pain.

Advice I

There are two sorts of advice givers: the advisor and the man-who-knows. A lot depends on your approach. If you are asking the questions, skipping and changing the subject, somehow controlling the agenda, then the person advising remains an advisor. Somehow you have to not care too much about the advice. If you do betray undue emotional identification with the subject (i.e., really care), then the advisor becomes the man-who-knows. You sit, puppy-like, as the pearls drop into your lap from the man's mouth. Hemingway loved this role. 'Papa' was the man-who-knows *par excellence*; even when he didn't know, he acted as if he did. Some men become so enamoured of being the man-who-knows that they contrive to turn as many encounters as they can into this kind of pearl-dropping format. The man-who-knows can adopt a certain persona that forces his interlocutor, almost against their will, into some kind of subservient advice-seeking humanoid. One method favoured by the man-who-knows is revelation of some kind of worrying, often medical or legal, information that personally affects the other. Having secured the position of power, 'owning' this sensitive, important info, the man-who-knows proceeds to dispense it in a fashion guaranteed to prolong the mentor-aspirant situation as long as possible. There is no sense of sharing in such an encounter, if the man-who-knows cannot be dominant he just won't play and will remain silent. To be 'polite' one gives the man-who-knows the kind of attention he craves. Because you don't want him to sulk. So the 'power', if you like, is dependent on who can stand the stink of bad personal relations best. The 'power' resides with the person who can stand confrontation, for whom confrontation holds no fears, or for whom confrontation never escalates, or for whom confrontation means very little.

Advice II

You might say it was about time I stopped asking all and sundry for advice about how to live my life. Even though, it is true, I am one of those people who need to have their views towards action vouchsafed by somebody else, even people who are absolutely unsuited to such a job. I am, you can see, something of a dream for what I call the bogus man-who-knows. But I've found that even bogus men-who-know know *something*, it's just that they are always over-extending themselves into areas where they don't know anything. Once you can recognise when someone knows what they're talking about you can learn those things and forget the rest.

The Photographer's Story

Martin was the kind of guy who would have been fat at school but was now just acceptably well built and bulky. I could not help noticing that every one of his bags was plastered with Camel Trophy stickers. Stupidly, I asked him why. We then spent most of the flight to Spain with him talking and me asking interested questions about his time covering the world's toughest off-road rally.

'But it can't be that tough, can it?' I said. 'I mean, they're in cars, aren't they?'

Martin gave me a good six reasons why the Camel Trophy was akin, in toughness, to a kind of cross between climbing Everest and escaping from Colditz. I exaggerate, a little, but the general effect was of him establishing his macho credentials whilst every time I brought up some little escapade of my own, just for a small, perfectly acceptable bit of bragging, he would suddenly lose interest and start tapping away at his laptop. 'Work,' he said, mingling apology and pride nicely.

Work! Here I was on a plane, possibly on my way to being

gored and tossed, and my sole companion wanted to work! This was a bad start.

We were in the smoking section and he asked for a cigarette. That was not a problem since I'm not, nor ever have been, one to dissuade bumming fags. But then he came out with an extraordinary: 'I never buy cigarettes, it's my way of giving up.'

'So you just bum them off other people, then?' I had to say. But he just grinned. Water off a duck's back.

Then there was the money. Earlier I had discovered he had no Spanish money, only his credit cards. 'What are you going to buy cigarettes with?' I asked. He just grinned. Now I knew why.

Pull yourself together, I said to myself. He's only the photographer.

I'd had this trouble before. Photographers who work for macho men's magazines, and writers too, for all I know, tend to act as if they work for a macho men's magazine. Their talk is all football, girlfriends and video games, peppered with the catchphrase of the moment, usually derived from some execrable TV show.

Martin was not interested in football, but he made up for it by being interested to a boyish and unhealthy degree in cars, especially off-road cars. When I mentioned, casually, that I had written a book he immediately told me in great detail about the book he'd written called *Landcruiser*, detailing every Toyota Landcruiser ever made in six continents over thirty-five years.

'Still in print?' I asked.

'Oh yes. In fact, it's something of a bestseller in Norway.'

I laughed my harsh barking laugh which I reserve for such situations, but he just gave me the duck's-back look.

'Oo. Looks like we're commencing descent. Game on,' he said, buckling up.

Martin was the kind of guy who would always be first to notice when the plane was descending, ascending or levelling. He would use the correct jargon for everything: 'slip' instead of 'road that joins the main road'; 'multicore cable' instead of 'flex'; 'radials' instead of 'tyres'; 'commencing descent' instead of 'landing'; 'powerful understeer' instead of 'flung off out of the corner'; 'brake nipple' instead of 'place where you put the oil in', and numerous other examples.

Jargon

It was Martin who made me understand that my own dedication to plain talking was in fact an admission of machismic failure. Ability to use jargon is one of the magic talismans of 'being a man' in the lousy modern world.

Of course, it has ancient parallels, of a sort. Being taught the secret magical language of the tribe or learning school jargon, as each new boy at Eton is forced to do. To my mind, though, it is a phoney substitute for real knowledge and a displacement of the real clue-giving language of men, which by the way they talk about discomfort, adventure, injury and death tells you a lot about the man.

Only those who can dispense with jargon have really mastered their subject, that was my view.

Male jargon: I never really got the hang of it even at school. It involved a delicate balance between knowing the right names for things but not knowing too much. For example, a too thorough knowledge of engines becomes too much like science. This is where the phoneyness comes in. It is as if the man involved only wants to know the right words and labels rather than get to the reality underneath.

Such a man, when a topic is raised, will drop in the jargon words he knows for no other or better reason than that he knows these words. In this idiom, jargon is the go-faster stripe of language, a useless decoration that implies superior performance.

The problem is, I am rather impressed by people who know the right words for everything. By this I mean of course the right techno-jargon words used in advertisements and manuals and not actually the words used even by people who might be expected to know them, such as shop assistants and mechanics.

My deep seated objection to these jargon words does not extend in any way to people who use the right words for parts of a horse or varieties of plants and trees. I can see the point of it there.

And if you are going to use jargon there is a way to do it which is apologetic, or, if that isn't your style, at least explanatory, in a way that does not belittle the listener. Martin used jargon words swiftly and expertly without explanation. Quite against my will I found myself asking him for clarification – this usually resulted in several more jargon words. The small comfort of knowing he didn't know what he was talking about was more than offset by the jarring realisation that he was convinced he was 'the better man'.

And wasn't I?

But without being confrontational I couldn't tell him he was also a wimp, obsessed by consumerist bollocks, narrow minded, and . . . and . . . a cigarette thief!

From the outset he presented bullfighting as something mad, and therefore I was not macho, simply mad.

The night before my run-in with the cow we had steaks in the draughty restaurant in the hotel where we were staying, miles from anywhere. I drank several Soberano brandies, but Martin was not with me. He said he wanted an early night.

'Look, it's me that's going in the ring with that thing, not you,' I said. He gave me his duck's-back look and reached for another cigarette.

11.00 p.m.

I can do nothing except sit and watch the heartbeat machine. The baby's heart fluctuates between a dizzy 160 and a crawling 65 – this is OK, apparently. I have now met the doctor in charge. She is younger than me, full of bounce and a phoney hail-fellow-well-met bonhomie, a bit like a vet before he shoves his hand up a cow's arse. But we aren't in a field in Yorkshire, we're in a dingy little delivery suite that opens off a low-roofed, white-walled corridor of such suites. On my way back from another cigarette I could hear the screams coming from behind each shut door as I walked past. Christ, if I didn't know something was being born I would have sworn I was walking down a corridor in a Gestapo jail.

We aren't in a field, yet the young doctor is talking to me as if I'm Farmer Giles and my wife is the cow: 'Let's just have a little look now'; 'Shall we get her on to her side now?' The young female doctor has not noticed my expensive shirt and shiny shoes in the gloom of the dirty little 'suite'. To her I am just another oik to be processed. I feel this very strongly and speak with clarity and a few long words. But I realise language in this place is for placating, fobbing off; all the 'choices' and 'questions' are just like those of a salesman, designed to get you running like a rabbit down to the one and only choice.

She announces, 'We're going to give the "little one" a "nick" in his scalp.'

'What on earth for?'

'To see if it's distressed.'

'Won't sticking a needle into its head distress it further?'

'No, actually we find they rather like it.'

She actually said this. I could only fume. Why didn't I know more? Why did it all feel as if something was about to go badly wrong?

It seemed that though my wife was dilating it wasn't happening fast enough. Who decided how fast it should happen? It seemed to be agreed. But from the moment we arrived nothing had happened 'fast enough'. Everything was a rush. Suddenly the swings on the heartbeat counter were taken as a bad sign, whereas previously they hadn't been anything much at all. 'The baby is distressed,' announced young doc, firmly, having got the measure of me.

'Hold on,' I said, 'couldn't we just pause for just a moment, catch our breaths, and examine all the options?'

Bitchily quick she snapped, 'We can turn off the heartbeat machine if you want. We can turn everything off, if you want?'

'Now hold on,' I said, putting on my most reasonable voice, but my wife cut in.

'Let me have a Caesarean,' she said, her face bleary and weary and strained and strange looking.

The young doctor beamed and I knew all along that this was the preferred plan – a nod at natural birth but really we're all much better off with the knife, with medical technology rather than human effort.

I looked at my wife and I remembered that innocuous remark, so long ago, from the specialist who 'recommended' the induction because my wife's blood sugar level was 'a tad high', and yet later other doctors had raised an eyebrow at this as if to say, what are we doing, having an induction? And I said nothing, and I said nothing now.

Game On

It was pouring with rain when Franc turned up at our hotel. He'd driven all the way from Madrid with a TV crew from Manchester and a woman radio reporter from the BBC. He also had arranged that two bullfighting critics, also from Madrid, were to come and observe. Franc would be fighting a bull and I would be fighting a cow. We looked at the bull ring. Part of it was under water. Franc didn't like it. He explained, and I could see why, that the cape becomes too heavy when it's raining. This makes it difficult to manipulate, possibly dangerous, as the cape sticks to the bull's back and doesn't fly up properly when it is charged.

I had to admire Franc blowing off all those people he had invited to come and watch him perform. That took courage too. He wasn't going in that ring unless the odds were on his side. He had nothing to prove. He had been gored before and yet had gone back into the ring and fought again with courage. They say a bullfighter is only really a bullfighter after he has been gored. It is how he faces the bull after a goring that counts.

I, though, had something to prove. The cows we had looked at, Franc assured me, were tiny. They looked big enough to do me considerable harm, and they had horns. Big, sharp, very bull-like horns.

The ring I would fight the cow in was more of a corral than a proper bull ring. In each corner there were rough oak-planked *barreras* to hide behind when the bull, or cow, charged. In the middle it was soggy underfoot, with a puddle like a Somme crater filled with water.

Franc and a wily young lad of about seventeen selected a reddish-coloured cow for me to 'fight'. I hid behind the *barrera* and took my 'sports' glasses off. I would have to face this one as a blur.

The lad of seventeen warmed the cow up for me by doing a few passes with his cape. At first the cow was skittery, but then it started to charge properly.

Behind the *barrera* I felt myself gearing up for the challenge. All my self-deprecation, jokes, lack of seriousness to cover my fear, went in those few minutes. Suddenly I was all business. Could I see without the glasses? Yes, certainly when it came into range. When it was my turn I was geared up and ready to fight. Not waiting for the cow but wanting to take the fight to the cow. It stood looking quizzically across at me over the huge pool of water.

'Go forwards!' shouted Franc.

I started to edge around the pool.

'No. Forwards!'

I squelched into the muddy shallows. The cow waited. I shouted at the cow. I wanted to show the cow who was boss. Unfortunately the shout was very loud and sounded like a skinhead 'Oi!'. But I wasn't worried about that because the cow was charging. Fast.

By what seemed like a miracle the beast went for the dangling red cape. I swept it over its back and prepared for its counter-charge. Even though the cow tried to turn sharply I had stepped forward and was out of the way when it charged again. On the third pass it carried past the cape and charged into my leg just above the knee. I felt its force then and knew I could master it. This was not a huge bull. It was fast and aggressive but not, after all, so very frightening. A few more *suerte*, with Martin clicking like mad outside the ring, and we were done.

Franc said, 'I must say you've got bollocks, my lad. Three passes you made out there. Three passes is all you need to call yourself a matador.'

I felt hugely pleased that Franc had given my *cojones* the thumbs up.

Martin said, 'What was all that shouting about?'

'That was aikido,' I said.

'Bloody cow understood whatever it was,' said Franc, with a certain heat, backing me up against the implied slur of Martin's comment.

It was very muddy leaving, but Martin was able to use his off-road driving skills to get us out safely and this cheered him up.

All's Well

Martin drove very fast and got us to the airport in good time. This fast driving and the earlier off-road stuff had given him a chance to strut his stuff. This balanced my exploits in the ring. That's all it had taken. Now we were firm friends, planning all sorts of articles together. I'd do the crazy stuff, he'd do the driving. That's all it took.

On the way we stopped for a quick drink in a deserted bar. Our two brandies sat on the high counter as we replayed the cow-fighting scene. Even though it was nearly winter there was sun everywhere in the bar. The brandy caught and magnified this warm feeling of danger avoided, an adventure concluded, a

Hemingway feeling if ever there was one: back on the safe path again with a drink after a deviation you can talk about. All that made it worth it, and, not surprisingly, all was right with the world.

Access Denied

In the end, after all the planning, and covert meetings and false names and attempts to convert me to radical policies of change involving bombs and assassination, Andy went without me. Or rather, he went to Assam, rather than Nagaland, and, conveniently, Assam wasn't a place I was interested in. Andy came back after two weeks having been under fire yet again, pursued by government forces for sixty hours non-stop through the jungles and tea gardens. It was exciting stuff, and just knowing Andy and hearing his story seemed enough. Going out to get shot at, just for the experience, I knew then I wasn't going to do it. I'd found my danger level, and that was above it. I'd settle for something I had more control over.

12.21 a.m.

I am wearing silly green surgeon's gear and plastic wellies. The porter who kitted me out has five kids and a second job driving a hearse. I didn't really want to hear that. I knock the side of my head to touch wood in this place of plastic and steel. My wife has been wheeled through to 'theatre'. As soon as it was agreed I noticed a real lightening up. It was as if control had returned to the experts. The weird mysterious human had been defeated – now we were going to do it the real way, the clean way, with the knife.

My wife is on a high trolley, made of gleaming stainless steel, and is hooked up to a central electronic console that looks like something for communicating with the space shuttle. The anaesthetist is there, the registrar, the young doctor, the midwife

– all subtly changed now they are be-masked and be-gowned, but I recognise them one by one as if we are survivors of some long and arduous party. Except it is all deadly serious, despite the chit chat about other people, as the young doc sorts through the tool roll of cutters.

They have drawn a decorous curtain across my wife's midriff; neither she nor I will be able to see what is going on behind this veil of mysteries. My wife can feel nothing below her waist and is showing her fortitude by smiling gamely. I clasp her hand and hold on tight. I dislike blood and I'm squeamish – I had already planned to duck out of any come-here-and-watch nonsense if it had been a normal birth, and I'm certainly not going to allow my eyes to waver even slightly towards the edge of the curtain, where I might just catch a horrible glimpse of something. I hold my wife's hand and look at her and she smiles gamely and somehow it feels like we're the last teenage lovers on the planet before it all goes up in flames. I feel so innocent. So in their hands. When will it all be over?

'There is nothing like a dame . . .' I am sure I can hear the registrar humming that on his breath, but I've been holding my ears, so to speak, so as not to catch any nasty sounds. I absolutely do not want to faint, which may be a possibility, because I'm untested in this field. I did faint, aged eight, when my sister threw a dart that stuck in my back just above my backside, and I pulled it out like Custer extracting an arrow. But, come on, that was a long time ago, though somehow it doesn't seem so now.

My grandfather was away at war when his son was born. My father was down the pub, came home a little tight, hugged the midwife and handed her a bottle of pale ale. I was clinging to my wife's hand cursing modernity and yet—

The clear accelerating sound of a baby's first yowl. Held up above the plastic curtain, a boy, and I'm ready of course for the sight of his tackle, bigger than you might expect, but then it always is at birth. Not being born, but untimely ripped, he is quite perfectly beautiful, I can see that objectively. I feel his eyes wide open and staring at everything, interested in everything already. I know, too, how to quell his screaming, read about it in a book about the Yananomi tribe: just walk the child, faster than a normal walk if necessary, but walk him and he will be calm.

I take up my precious bundle and start to pace and pace faster and soon enough he stops his crying. At long last I feel I've done something right, proved a tiny, obscure point. Those tribes know something and I explain all this to the bemused anaesthetist, shake everyone's hands, haven't really forgiven them, but I can still say thank you, and return the boy (7½ lbs) to his mum.

The Tribe

Finally, I was going to meet the tribe. They weren't a lost tribe, but they weren't that well known either. They were former headhunters and I had interested a TV company in making a film about the snakehunting exploits of these people, the Huaoulu. The TV company had been excited by my book *Big Snake*, and they wanted me, with the tribe's help, to catch a snake longer than thirty feet.

The Huaoulu are that increasingly common kind of 'remote' tribe that are now relatively easy to get to. Four days from Jakarta and you can be deep in the jungle with these former headhunters, who wear red headbands if they are warriors. This suited the film, because it was picturesque. They were also reputed to be good at hunting. Their island home, Seram, was famous for giant snakes. It was the director's hope that the tribe's hunting skills could be directed at catching a record-breaking serpent.

The village was on a muddy hillside less than a kilometre inside virgin forest. Selective logging had taken its toll elsewhere, mainly in the rutted, flooded tracks left by caterpillar bulldozers. When we walked we often passed trees with plastic discs nailed to them; these were valuable trees the logging company scouts had earmarked for felling. Whenever we passed such a tree Tjep, our Westernised translator, would tear the disc off and fling it away. After a while we all started doing this. The Huaoulu used to laugh when they saw this. The logging company were no friends of the tribe, though they were too frightened to tear off the discs themselves.

The King's Problem

The king of the tribe was a wily old devil. His face could go from benign, even obsequious, piety one minute to a face of rocky hardness the next. If he didn't want to answer he didn't – and why shouldn't he? He was the king, after all. He was dogged by only two things: his idiot son and the activities of a Japanese pearling company in their traditional sago groves. The company had claimed the sago as theirs and the Huaoulu were disputing this. The idiot son was merely greedy, almost to the point of madness, and was intoxicated by all things Western. Since the king was also a visionary worker of magic it galled him that his son was interested only in superficial fripperies. Towards the end of our stay the king asked us if anyone wanted to learn his magical skills. He said a German had stayed with him six years but had left just before the king could pass on the final secret. I seriously considered turning myself into a shamanic sidekick, but only for about ten seconds. I could just about imagine six months living with the Huaoulu, but not six years.

Sweeteners For the Tribe:

50kg bag of sugar. Two 50kg bags of rice. 10kg rough tobacco. Twelve Chinese red plastic torches. 10kg salt. 5000 Gudam Garam cigarettes. Several transparent plastic sheets. Assorted blue polyester ropes. Batteries. A blue paper carton of matches.

We also had to pay them a fee, which we negotiated through Tjep. Mysteriously, every night we had to renegotiate the fee a little higher, a little higher. By the time we set off for the great snake hunt we were due to pay them a lot of money.

The Jungle Crouched

Moving through the jungle. You wake up and it's raining. Being careful not to slide off the sleeping platform or drop any dry item into the churned mud below you start to swap dry sleeping clothes for cold, damp walking clothes. Dry sleeping shirt off, damp, muddy vest, which is so stretched it barely covers both nipples, on. Dry tracksuit pants off, wet combat trousers on. Then wet socks and wet boots. Time for a cigarette and a stand by the fire. It is still dark.

Seram is benign rainforest. Mosquitoes are only a bother at night and then not really very bad. I've suffered much worse mossie attacks in southern France. By day it is only the heavy intermittent rain that is a drag. But as soon as you start walking the wet clothes steam up and start to feel warmish. My jungle boots with built-in pump action are the triumph of the trip. We wade through so many rivers it becomes impossible to keep taking boots off. Everyone else gets blisters on their damp, soft feet, but mine remain pumped gloriously dry. The boots are ex-US army, developed for Vietnam – at least they did something right out there.

Tarzan

The forest is up and down, up and down, wet leaves and mud under foot, huge multi-buttressed trees and dark green light. The vines that hang down are all strong enough to take Tarzan. In fact, it's the buttressed trees and heavy vines that make the jungle different from an ordinary wood in Western Europe.

Lea and Perrin's

The Huaoulu are terrible cooks. Or rather the cook that cooks for us is a terrible cook. The meat, which is always deer or monkey or cassowary, is either incredibly chewy or pongy and going off. Everyone is glad that I brought Worcester sauce with me and everyone, even Tjep, asks for a shot on their meat before chowing down to their meal.

The chef is a camp transvestite. He simpers, wears red lipstick and has several dangly ear rings in each ear. He is the only man allowed into the women's quarters of the king's house, which is the largest house in the village. All the houses are high off the ground, made of split not sawn logs, and have a large open verandah part and an enclosed women's section.

We learn that the camp chef is also head of the young men's house.

Another transvestite we nickname Moses because of his lengthy white beard. He wears women's dark glasses, long dangly ear rings and a plastic jewelled ring on his thumb. He is very affectionate and charming and has several grandchildren. We learn that he was once also head of the young men's house.

Tjep explains that the prevailing Indonesian culture that the tribe experience, meeting loggers and officials down at the sea, is one of contempt for homosexuality. The tribe are therefore sheepish about the homosexual phase that the young men go through when they live in the young men's house before they get married.

Naturally, the discovery that the young men who are carrying our equipment may also be gay causes quite a stir amongst the team, despite our world-traveller liberal pretensions. Tjep proves the most parochial on the subject. He is also offended by the tribe's lack of hygiene, the fact that the kids wander around with bare arses crapping anywhere.

'Do you think we're going to get sick here?' asks the soundman.

The Tribe Decide

The tribe aren't easy to push around, despite having been promised a huge sum of money if they catch us a giant snake – alive, we keep repeating. On the first day that we're supposed to start filming the men of the village assemble at around seven-thirty ready to help. The director, like all directors everywhere, is not ready. The crew are used to waiting for him to set up shots, etc., but the villagers aren't. After hanging around for about half an hour they all disappear into the forest to go trapping, machete polishing, searching for bark. When the director announces he's ready there is no one to film. Even the king is unavailable. He is 'resting' (i.e., asleep). Which is not surprising since he was still up chewing betel nut at three-thirty when I went to bed.

It filters back that the tribesmen think we're not serious because we didn't keep to the set start time. So much for the idea that indigenous peoples are just sitting around waiting for the white man to waste their time. The king has also announced that any hunting must be preceded by a ceremony, for which we have already paid. Unfortunately, he says the time has to be right for a ceremony otherwise it won't work.

I Get To Demonstrate My Archery Skills

Several days go by in which we do very little except have archery lessons, first from Moses, who is such a terrible shot that both Tjep and I hit the tree stump target more often than he does, and then, after Moses went off in a huff, with the top hunter of the village, who is, it must be admitted, a first-rate archer. The arrows are about six feet long, with no flights and no notch in the end of the arrow. These are primitive arrows, almost like those made by kids from garden bamboos. Only the tips are sophisticated. They range from fish arrows with serrated edges to bodkin-like points to arrows that have a channel to take poison.

Before I met such a tribe that lived by hunting, fishing and trapping I had always thought that everyone would be good at hunting. But just like any cross-section of people, some members of the tribe are good at it and some are not so good.

Though there is plenty of male-being activity for the tribesmen – hunting, trapping, building huts – I am conclusively not able to discover if there is any rite of passage any more. In the king's youth they still took heads, though that stopped in the 1950s. The hunter tells us that men have to spear a wild boar before they are considered men and are therefore entitled to the red hat of the tribal warrior, but Moses says that men become men when they get married, and that's when they wear the red hat.

The king's son wears the red hat and he's a complete dickhead – sly, ignorant (he has to ask the other tribesmen for the name of an insect we are interested in), obsessed by Western technological gadgets and threatening when he thinks he isn't getting his way. I have a feeling that even here the rite of passage cuts less ice than owning a Toyota Landcruiser.

The Right Moment

Once the king had established that nothing would happen until the moment was right for the ceremony he did not need to hide and spent most days and a lot of the night lounging around chatting on his platform, which was a raised part on three sides of his verandah.

Earlier that day we had finished filming another archery lesson. Our teacher was sitting at the king's house when he reached into the rafters and pulled a bunch of dry grass down that was stuffed there. Quickly, using thumb, forefinger and his thigh as a rolling board, he began to twine a perfectly even piece of thin rope. This was the way all bow strings were made. We all tried weaving the string from the grass. The man laughed in a friendly manner at our efforts. Then the king joined in and showed off his rolling skill. Then I asked if they still made fire using bamboo fire ploughs, which I believed was the ancient way. The king said they had been using flint and steel for as long as he could remember, though he said he could also use bamboo. He reached into his little woven box (all the men had one of these containing useful oddments) which he carried over his shoulder. He took out flint, a piece of dark metal and a bundle of lint-like material. Laying the tinder material down he started striking sparks with a vengeance. Finally one landed. He then held up the tinder in that supplicatory tenderness I knew from my own firelighting experiments. The glowing smoking tinder was placed inside some of the grass used to make the bow string. Blown upon and tended to carefully it suddenly burst into flames, whereupon a grimy candle from the box was lit. We all lit clove cigarettes off the candle. The king beamed.

Suddenly the king pulled us all into a circle and said, let's make a ceremony. We dutifully chewed betel nut leaves and waited as the king intoned a prayer to the spirits of the forest.

Then he handed out bracelets woven out of special grass stems. 'Wear it until you cross the sea,' said the king, 'and no harm will come to you.'

It was all over quite quickly. We could now go. The king entered a brief trance to find out the best place for us to look for the snake. Previously there had been talk of going north, towards a large swamp. Instead he said we should head south, towards some hilly ground beyond the river. There we would find the big snake, he was quite certain. And we did.

Mature

The interesting part was that our genuine admiration for the making of fire led to the right kind of atmosphere for a ceremony. We had gone to the tribe like brash tourists who have paid a lot of money and want, nay demand, their full dollars' worth. The waiting around slowly burnt that out and the admiration for the firemaking reversed the situation. Instead of demanding something from the tribe we had reached a situation of parity, a non-greed situation, a sharing situation, if you like, and sensing this, for once, non-commercial atmosphere, the king made his ceremony, since I guess such ceremonies are pointless if made under the wrong conditions.

The tribe had an emotional flexibility far beyond ours, were able to switch apparent mood with ease, which, combined with an emotional sensitivity like that of young children, made it easy for them to out-manoeuvre us. I won't say the tribe were wise, but they were certainly more than a match for four hard-nosed television makers and a writer from the safe West.

Making Fire

I was able to learn from Ray Mears, one the world's top teachers of 'survival', how to make fire using primitive technology. I didn't think it would be that useful but it is something I had always wanted to learn. Mears taught me how to start a fire using a stiff bow strung with parachute cord that wound once around an inch-thick pencil-shaped 'drill'. The top of the drill was very pointed and sat in a hardwood cup, a small block with a depression cut into it as a bearing for the drill end. The bearing was lubricated with a holly leaf crushed up. The other end was much more rounded, so as to maximise friction, and this, with its shallow point, sat in another carved depression in the 'hearth board'. Every piece of the kit was made from the same kind of wood, in our case, dead, dry (but not rotten) sycamore. Clematis and ivy wood make more combustible drills, but are not as easy to make.

The drill is rotated by the bow string which goes around it and, as you 'saw' backwards and forwards, converts this motion into rotation. The other end soon gets hot and starts to smoke and burn a black hole into the hearth. When the hole is deep enough to take the end of the drill and its shallow sides, but not so deep as to fit the straight part of the drill barrel, you must cut a notch one eighth of the area of the circle of the drill hole that extends like a wedge of cheese right to the edge of the board. Then you start to drill in earnest.

This is the hard part. It took me three days to learn, in rainy, humid conditions, but I can still do it. It is not a skill you forget.

The drilling produces a dark brown dust that gathers in the notch and starts to smoke. In that fragile dustball resides a microcoal, glowing red, about the size of a big pin head.

On a dry leaf or chip of wood transfer the dustball with its coal very carefully to your face and gently blow until a continuous stream of smoke is apparent. Better, let a natural breeze excite such smoke. The really hard part is now to transfer the coal on its chip into the birdsnest heart of a combustible ball you have made from stripped and separated clematis, very dry grass, long dry pine needles, the thin furly curly dry bark of a silver birch: anything very dry and very combustible into the heart of which you place the coal. Then blowing on it and giving it between breaths time to recover, rather like resuscitating a drowned man, you have to find, amazing as it sounds, the rhythm of that particular glowing coal, and when you've found it each breath will feed instead of quench its tiny fire until by some magic a threshold is crossed and the whole ball of tinder bursts into flame. It really does do this. The only warning you get is that smoke intensifies, pouring from the ball of tinder until, foof, it's all alight.

There must be few more satisfying feelings than lighting a fire from a flaming tinder ball you ignited through the skilful use of a drill and bow. It is as if a space has been cleared in your head when you realise you no longer are dependent on matches and other manufactured goods.

I imagine if you make a snare from woven grass stems and catch an animal that provides a meal you feel that same partial enlivening of the soul, that same liberation from the dead hand of modernity, dependence on the machine world.

Jaws

Coming back from Indonesia the wrong way, trying to prolong my adventures abroad, I found myself in Guam with a day in hand before flying on the next day. I decided to go dinghy sailing. I wanted to sail out into the place where the ships of the Japanese and American navies had fought. Coincidentally, the place I was sailing from was the last port of call for the *USS Indianapolis* before it was sunk at the very end of World War 2. The *Indianapolis* had carried the bomb across the Pacific. It had then set sail for the Philippines but had been sunk by a Japanese sub on the way. The huge battleship went down in twelve minutes. Eleven hundred men went into the sea. Five days later, when rescue eventually came, only three hundred were still alive.

In the movie *Jaws*, the Hemingwayesque shark hunter Quinn is supposed to be one of the survivors. He tells of the terrible tiger shark attacks that befell the shipwrecked men. Only half the survivors were on rafts, the rest just floated in the sea, supported by kapok life vests that slowly became waterlogged. During moments of hysteria in the night men would fight imaginary adversaries, or each other, for the lifejacket of a man who had died. To keep the sharks at bay the men joined into big circles and splashed and hit the water to drive off the hungry predators. Others claimed that resting quietly without movement was a better strategy for survival. In any case, and the film doesn't bring this out, as many men were lost from the extreme privation of being in the burning Pacific sun for five days without fresh water as were eaten by marauding sharks.

The Sea

The water was sparkly blue and the wind whipped off the flitting sawtooth waves into the blue terylene sail, stretching it to the full and powering the boat along at a fine speed. I'd get to that rock easily, far out in the bay with a few gulls, tiny white smudges rising and then abruptly falling down to the sea around it.

I sat out, experimentally at first, slipping my bare feet under the rough nylon toe straps. The boat heeled with a sudden smart breeze and I hung my backside over the edge to balance things, letting out the sail to ease pressure on the heeling boat. The sun-shrivelled excuse of a life vest I was wearing had a trapeze harness built into it. Feeling bold, I unclipped the wire that led from the top of the mast and clipped it into my harness. Now, when the wind blew, I didn't need to let out the sail and spill wind, I could stand right out on the side of the boat, keeping the craft upright, waves splashing up and soaking my arse from time to time, but that was all part of the fun. Sailing out of the bay I heard the deep vibrating hum of the boat as it rose up to plane on its own bow wave, literally surfing along, giving an impression of great speed.

The rock was as big as a house and waves crashed whitely around its base, less than a half a kilometre from the shore. My plan was to sail out and around this landmark, taking care, of course, not to get shipwrecked.

The cleats for the jib, the small sail at the front, had been set within reach of the helm, so the boat could be sailed, as I was doing, single-handed. To go about or tack I would need to release the jib rope so that it could flap freely, push the tiller across so that the boat turned abruptly into the wind and then the mainsail would follow, me ducking under it to get to the other side. The strong wind blowing off the sea and obliquely into the bay meant that over time I was being pushed into one side of the bay, which was distinctly rocky looking. In order to make a turn in the opposite direction, to gain distance away from the rocks, I would need to jib. Jibing is when instead of turning the front of the boat through the wind you turn the back of the boat. Instead of a gentle movement as the wind shifts from one side to the other, the sail wangs overhead with tremendous force. People are regularly killed by booms smacking into them on unforeseen jibs, though on boats far larger than mine, it must be said. But the aluminium boom of a fifteen-foot dinghy could give you a nasty headache, even knock you out if you were very careless.

I was starting to get close to the open sea, that point beyond the protection of the two headlands where the sea was rougher and a different colour, slate blue rather than green. The rock island loomed nearer and nearer, bigger than I thought, its top split like jagged teeth. I saw that by tightening the sail I could squeak past the headland and leave the island on my left. I wouldn't have to jib, after all.

As I neared this rougher water I saw that though the wind was stronger I could still easily sail here; there was a swell, but the bottom was deep and the only breaking waves were little white caps. My small dinghy easily climbed up and down each wave. It would have been sensible, perhaps, to turn back, while I was still well within my capabilities, circle the island as I had planned, but the situation was not dangerous and for the fun of it I decided to keep sailing out to sea.

There was a current, the old man on the beach who had rented me the boat told me, but nothing too strong. Sailing past the dominating bulk of the island I could see no seagulls, but I could hear strange bird cries over the crashing of waves. The water was greener and shallower here but plenty deep enough for the dinghy.

Out in the rougher sea I now had room to let the sail out and swoop along in a broad reach. I told myself, I'd return with a real ocean-going boat one day and sail all the way to Japan.

I was way past the rock now and the hut on the beach was only just visible. My backside was soaked through and my hands were red and raw from the unaccustomed rope work. To turn back I didn't really need to jib, but I was so confident I did, rather than sail an extra leg to make room for a normal turn. The jib was released and flapping. I pushed the helm over, the boom thwacked across and I just ducked in time, but then the boat started to heel. I tried to let out the mainsail but the rope had caught on the pulley slide at the stern. I just thought about going head to wind when I found myself falling into the sail. I was over, capsized.

I went under for a second, but my glasses were still on my face. Good, don't want to lose them. The water was surprisingly warm. My feet kicked crazily in a hyper-adrenalated treading of water. I kicked off both my fancy coloured flip-flops, bought that morning, better off without them. The water felt thin, incapable of supporting. 'Now,' I thought to myself calmy, 'you must not panic. You must do things, quietly and efficiently.' I had never capsized before and had only done the drill on a couple of occasions, when I was twelve. The theory came back to me instantly as I manoeuvred myself around the boat. A bigger than normal wave broke unpleasantly over my head. Don't want to lose my glasses. Very calmly I took them off and put them inside my buttonable saturated shirt pocket.

The theory was that I should grab the centre-board, which was sticking up like a shark fin, and pull on that with all my weight. Slowly the boat would begin to revert. When it was lying horizontal I should stand on the board and this should lift the sodden sail and mast from the sea. I should pull on the shrouds to steady myself and this would lift the boat upright again.

I lifted myself out of the water and grabbed the slimy board sticking three feet out from the boat bottom. At that point my eyes looked towards the beach and I could see that I was so far out that the hut was now behind the headland. The old man would not know that I had gone over. He would not then launch his twelve-foot aluminium skiff with a powerful outboard and come to my rescue. He was probably having a cup of tea right now, caring not a jot what happened to me. Behind me was sea, all the way to Japan.

Miraculously, the mast started to move sluggishly through the water. Part one was working. Some part of my brain had shut down, the conscious part that hoped or expected in public, on screen, as it were, but subconsciously the hoping went on and I knew my hope of success was not in vain, not yet.

I pushed down on the board and scrambled on to it, flexing it up and down with my weight, pulling at the same time on the handy rope that trailed, I guessed, from the jib cleat on the other side.

The boat began its majestic rise. Inside it was full of water, but the sloping sides contained buoyancy tanks, at least efficient enough for it not to sink.

The half-sunk boat began to catch the wind again. I tried getting in over the side but that made it heel too much so I went in over the stern. Just as I was safely in the flooded cockpit, I saw the sail strain from another gust. This sort of thing doesn't happen to me, I thought, as I saw the rope snag again – why had I forgotten to clear it? With horrible inevitability the boat heeled and heeled. Just before it went right over I plopped into the water to stop myself from being forced under. I was back in the drink again.

Now, risking a glance at the land, I could see that the wind or the current or probably both had taken me right past the mouth of the bay. I was now in the open sea, the open Pacific Ocean. I kicked my legs and thought for a vague second about sharks. If they came, would I lie still or hit the water? I didn't know. I deliberately stopped myself from thinking along these lines, concentrating on the job at hand, not frightened or panicking in the least, not really. I knew now I could lift the boat. I just had to do it again, though I noticed by the way I was treading water that I was a lot more tired than before. So much adrenaline had been pumped out in the first capsize that I'd been exerting myself to the maximum. Nevertheless, I did all the things I'd done before, but first clearing the rope off the snag at the back.

I lifted her, more slowly this time, and a lot more effort was needed on the initial tug on the centreboard, but she was up and then I was over the stern sorting out the ropes when the sail filled and this time the rope snagged inside the pulley, twisting up on itself. And I jibed again and went over again.

This time, when I surfaced, I was really tired. The water was cold, like English sea water, not tropical any more. More and more waves seemed to be breaking annoyingly over my head. If I didn't get it up this time I knew I wouldn't at all. I did not think about death or drowning. I curtailed all my thoughts into an icy stream of the purely necessary. My rapidly tiring body had just enough for one more attempt – that I knew with horrible certainty. So now I needed to be cunning.

Conserving my energy I manoeuvred the boat around while it was still in the water, pointing the bow head to wind. It had been foolish not to do this before, but only in my desperate state was I thinking 100 per cent clearly.

The boat lined up and I grabbed again for the centre-board and started the slow haul. I knew if I failed now I would have to lie on the top of the boat and hope for the best as I drifted out further and further. I thought about a story I read of how tanker crews were used to picking broken fishing boats out of the bow nets, boats run down without being noticed during the night. There were never any survivors.

The mast began to stir. Then it slowly moved. I was better now at deploying my weight. I shifted to the rope and stood on the board. Up at last came the boat. Instead of lunging straight back in I hung off the stern, positioning the boat again, making sure all the sails flapped harmlessly in the wind. I fixed the blocks at the back from my watery position and only then did I try to get aboard. It was a huge, lumbering, seal-like last effort, but there I was, jelly-like and exhausted, in the bottom of the boat.

I had time now to set the sails, to ease nervously back so that the wind would catch me. This time there would be no sitting out on the trapeze. Like a waterlogged animal I crouched on the floorboards of the boat peeping over the gunwhales to make my navigation decisions. The baler had been lost, but I was able, once the boat was moving, to open the two little perspex drain windows at the back. The boat emptied quite well.

I had to make one more jib to get inside the bay. I was nervous now. This time I couldn't make another mistake. Slackening all ropes off, but not to such an extent that a hanging length might get snagged, I rammed the tiller towards me to turn back through the wind. The boom whipped over, the sail filled but I was quick to let it slacken. Now I could sail in a line for the bay's entrance.

As I beached the boat, the small boy again appeared to help drag it up the beach. The old man was nowhere to be seen; he'd gone home for the day, the boy explained. I looked out to the horizon, to the rock island and the blue sea that stretched all the way to mainland Japan, full of sharks and supertankers. I was dog tired and cold and thinking slowly, and for a long time I watched the white birds again circling and dropping around the rock. White seabirds are ghosts of the ancestors, Chinese sailors used to say.

1.15 a.m.

My wife is sleeping. My son is sleeping. I am searching in the hospital car park for my car. Just as I am unlocking the door I search out where the window of my wife's ward should be, a darkened window high up on the sixth floor of the marble cliffs, which are still gleaming whitely in the moon light.

A man, apologetic, my age, glasses, nice shirt and clean pressed trousers, asks if he needs to buy a car park ticket. At this late hour! He has just dropped his wife off, contractions every four minutes. I give him my ticket and he's off to hold her hand. Good luck to him – no war to go to, no pub to hide in – just us and the marble cliffs. It's between the two of us now, and I drive off home fast, tooting my horn for no apparent reason.

Flight Plan

Flying back to London after my capsize experience the plane was rerouted over the very centre of town, following the Thames from the estuary up to Heathrow. Flying upriver, seeing the tiny toylike cars on each bank, the model trainset trees and the faintest of faint puff of smoke from a factory chimney far below, I felt a sudden realisation that the world was bigger than us antlike humans, that despite all the evidence of pollution we were actually making very little impact on the planet, that we were still just temporary visitors. My wife had just told me over the phone that she was pregnant. Now I was just getting used to the idea. With prescient certainty I somehow know that the kind of place my child will be living in will be less self-centred than the present world, since only in our heads is it a small sussed-out planet. Out there it is vast, humbling, unfathomable.

Bicycle Sufficiency

Sometimes, quite often, around six or seven on a summer evening, I take off on my mountain bike to practise wheelies and have fun riding across fields to the river.

I tend to practise wheelies when no one else is around, in empty streets, taking care not to crash into cars when I come off the back of the bike, which is often. If no one is around I don't feel at all silly trying to ride a bike on the back wheel alone. But if anyone is watching then I become self-conscious. I wasn't even sure I would write about it, since it didn't quite 'fit in' with the rest of the book, with its emphasis on difficulty and danger. Actually, wheelies *are* difficult, though not quite in the way of a rite of passage, sort of, but not quite. And practising wheelies is a kind of male-being activity, but not exactly, not without a bit of hedging and unpicking of the theory. But practising wheelies was one secret I wanted to reveal, even though I'm obviously not that proud of it.

Of course, I could update my childish need to wheelie by buying a motorbike, maybe an off-road bike. I could even organise a trip abroad, say, crossing a desert never before crossed on off-road bikes. Out there in the desert with only the nomads watching I could blow wheelies to my heart's content. Maybe I could even get sponsorship, perhaps raise money for charity.

Or I could avoid other people and just ride around the block. Flipping and flipping at the bars.

As a child I could never do wheelies. Kids at my school who studied hard, or were middle class, never could. But now, twenty or so years later, I'm getting there. The secret of wheelies, I'm learning, is to practise them going up a slight hill; somehow that aids balance. The second secret is to keep your centre of concentration not in the hands but in the feet. This shifts your centre of gravity lower, making balancing easier. Not thinking too much also shifts the centre lower. In fact, maybe the studious lads at school couldn't pull wheelies because their centre of gravity was too high; too much thinking.

When my father was thirty-five he had a house, a wife, three kids and went to work every day in his car. It is inconceivable to think of him doing what I'm doing, practising wheelies. In fact, though I've told no one, it's my summer project. By autumn I want to be the wheelie king of the neighbourhood. The secret wheelie king.

Kids around here can pick up on my anxieties. Once I pulled a little too hard, flipped off the back and the chain came off. As I bent down to fix it, two boys, who'd been a long way behind, overtook me. They said, just loud enough for me to hear but quiet enough to deny they'd said anything if I got annoyed, 'Shouldn't have been showing off.'

Thirty-five years old. Pulling wheelies. Or rather not pulling wheelies. Incurring the scorn of not-even teenagers. What's going on?

Grown men kick footballs around in parks. It's the same thing. Having fun. Keeping fit. Looking a prat, but who cares?

I've never liked football, never been any good at it, so I stay away from the kick-arounds and even affect to despise them, but, really, we're no different.

One thing that is different now is that grown men aren't that shy about doing juvenile things: wheelies, football, frisbee, combat-kite flying.

The difficult juvenile things are less and less popular: serious bike racing, model-aircraft flying, model-boat building, ham radio. These serious hobbies seem too complicated, and, besides, no one has time for them now what with work, TV, computer games, the Net.

There is also an element of professionalism in the serious hobbies which I think many men want to get away from. This professionalism has already taken over their work lives. They want a bit of a break. Pulling wheelies is something I can do on my own. I don't need to go on a course, get a licence, be judged or tested in some way. But the cost of this escape from the constricting grasp of professionalism is a return to the infantile. So I do my wheelies in private.

And slowly I'm getting there. It's actually not nearly as difficult as I used to think.

The Spiral Path

A Japanese calligraphy teacher told me that a path to knowledge doesn't go in a straight line, it goes in a spiral, round and around, constantly crossing the same turf again and again, but each time moving a little further out, getting a wider perspective, seeing the same thing from a different viewpoint. He made many spiral brush strokes on the handmade paper to emphasise his point. 'Like spider's webs,' he said. 'Like a seashell. Like double helix of DNA. It is a pattern of the living thing.'

The Stars

Six weeks on now and I've hardly done anything to my shed. I've been bonding with my son. Though it sounds ludicrous, such early bonding does happen. There is, it seems to me, a certain critical amount of time you have to spend each day holding the infant and suddenly it clicks in and you feel you know what he's going to do next and he no longer seems an unpredictable little bundle designed solely to cause anxiety and frustration. We have also been learning the bad side of a Caesarean – because my wife has had to be very careful about the healing scar she has not been able to carry our son. So she has not, and she tells me this, felt she has really bonded with him. So my gain has been her loss, all of it stemming, I still feel, from something beyond our control. The men run the hospital and the man is now holding the baby and the woman is lying there with a big cut in her stomach, but it is healing well, it is healing.

My wife is indoors reading or watching the news on television. Today was a sunny day and as we still haven't returned Dave's oil drum I lit a barbecue fire just for us. It is night now and the embers in the half drum are still glowing redly, and every now and then some sort of surface event on a piece of charcoal results in a tiny sparkle of white light.

Though I've hardly done anything to the shed I've started planning my next project. I was thinking first about Polynesian star sailors navigating without charts and that brought me to thinking about Polynesian catamarans and there, right in front of me, was the solution: build a boat instead of dreaming about affording one; build it in the garden, but in two parts, two three-foot-wide hulls that can be joined together after fitting them through the tiny gap between the suburban houses. Four foot eight inches wide and thirty-five feet long, way big enough to make an ocean-going vessel.

There is a moon, a few days away from being full, lodged in

the eucalyptus tree that overhangs our garden from next door. Above that is the night sky, full of stars.

Sitting inside the foundations of my shed I can rest my back against one of the upright poles and stare at the night sky. Two or three aeroplanes go by, looking at first like UFOs, using the lights of the town as a landmark.

The intersection of the rafters makes a star shape above me but, as there is no roof, I can see through the gaps at eight segments of night sky. I feel that I am in an ancient observatory, the kind used by the Egyptians and Persians before telescopes were invented. It is dark at the end of the garden, far from the sodium streetlighting that sends up a fuzzy light, spoiling one's view of the heavens.

In my observatory I sip from a bottle of wine and note the stars: Cassiopeia, Orion, the Plough just dipping below the horizon, the same stars I learned from books and from my father when I was a little boy. The same stars that have always graced the sky, always been the companions of the human race.

I'm staring so hard at the heavens, trying to make out Rigel and the Dog Star, that the tiny pinpricks of light above start to detach themselves and come towards me. It is as if the sky is now only a few metres above me, as if I can reach out and touch the blackness and the holes in the blackness that are letting in light.

It strikes me that the ancient idea that the stars are merely holes in a black firmament, holes that let in the vast light behind, seems a sensible idea. This vast light we have to be protected from – it is far too bright for our poor human eyes.

For a while I have the strongest impression of the connectedness of all things, that these connections between things are more important than the things themselves. I see each tree joined to each tree and each star, as if I can almost see the relationship between them.

The same stars above, whatever we may do or think. The holes in a dark firmament letting through light. Instead of seeing the night as only darkness, I see the night as increasingly full of stars, presentiment of dawn and the great awakening provided by the sun.